THEN MY LIVING SHALL NOT BE IN VAIN

THE LIFE LEARNINGS
OF
ORLEAN WILSON DUBUCLET

DORRANCE
PUBLISHING CO
EST. 1920
PITTSBURGH, PENNSYLVANIA 15235

EUNICE GILES MORGAN WALKER

Dorrance Publishing Co
585 Alpha Drive
Pittsburgh, PA 15238
Visit our website at dorrancebookstore.com

ISBN: 978-1-6480-4276-8
eISBN: 978-1-6470-2613-4

Then My Living Shall Not Be In Vain

I just did not come to this earth to take up space but to help others and accomplish something in this life however small.

Orlean Wilson Dubuclet

Foreword

*N*ot often is there an opportunity to comment on the story of a life so well lived or have the privilege to personally witness some of that story in real time. There could be no greater tribute paid to Orlean Wilson Dubuclet, a woman of ninety-six years, than a book about her life. Orlean did not just live on the fringes of life but lived by full immersion in a life driven by purpose.

On this purpose-filled journey as Rudyard Kipling penned, she has met both "triumph and disaster and treated these two imposters just the same."

The Life of Orlean Dubuclet still being lived provides insight into her favorite mantra "Where there is a Will, there is a WAY."

As I sat with Orlean listening to her life story, I was struck by how consistent and long term her commitment to helping others has been. Even at age ninety-six, she continues to be a Self-Ordained financial and motivational consultant to anyone asking her advice or frankly to anyone who will listen.

This attitude of "I am my brother's keeper" started early in life. There is evidence of this during her childhood and early adulthood. In the '50s she founded an organization (The Cooperettes, Inc.) to help delinquent youths. Her dedication and commitment to the Community through the Unity Project, designed to create new black businesses in South Central in the 1960s, extracted personal sacrifices. She also found ways not only to enlarge the lives of her own children but neighborhood children as well.

What is equally as impressive is how she never lost sight of her childhood dream of owning a women's dress shop and becoming a successful entrepreneur.

When it was time to pass the torch around age eighty-seven, she still found a way to be relevant by involving herself in the activities of her grand and great-grandchildren, and by encouraging neighbors on her morning walks, and others over the telephone. Orlean has gotten older but not "old." She remains vibrant, keeping abreast of current events in business and politics.

Orlean has an abiding faith and believes that she has always had the favor of God in her life, even during challenging times, which is a theme you will find throughout this book.

March 2019

Eunice Giles Morgan Walker

Contents

Introduction

I like saying that I was not put on this earth to just take up space but to accomplish something or make some kind of contribution even if in the smallest way.

At age ninety-six at the printing of this book, I believe I have learned something that I can share of my life's experiences that might be of some help to somebody. So after each chapter of my book I share what I have learned.

My basic mantra has always been "where there is a will there is a way" and of course one which Mama always had me to repeat "I can, I will, and I must."

The title of this book could just as easily had been titled "Where there is a will there is a way" or God's favor.

This is not a "tell all book" but my own account of my life experiences that perhaps may be of some value not just to my own family but to the many other wonderful family members I have acquired along the way.

I have tried to reference some of the material in the text so as to provide some historical context of the time in which it occurred for younger readers.

Finally, early in life "I found favor" in so many ways, even when the experiences could have been bad or especially challenging, so at an early age I came to feel God's presence and believe that God's hand was always guiding me, therefore the wind has always been at my back.

As long as I live, I will continue to pursue my purpose of not allowing my living to be in vain and not just take up space on this earth but contribute something.

Chapter 1

Beginnings

Events Surrounding My Birth

Both my name and birth year are still to this day in need of verification for authenticity. For sure I was born on Christmas Day either 1923 or 1924. The doctor and midwife attending my home birth in Good Pine, the small Louisiana town where I was born, evidently did not file a record of my birth. I don't know if it was because they were reeling from almost losing my mother in childbirth or whether they were just celebrating the holidays too much.

It was Christmas Day and Mama was so close to death from delivering an eighteen (some say twenty) pound baby that it took her months to recover. So between the two phenomena, my birth may have never been recorded. Daddy was sure it was December 25, 1924; Mama says it was December 25, 1923. However, I have chosen to use December 25, 1923 as my official date of birth.

Mama said that because of my unusual birth weight people came from near and far to see me. The picture I saw of myself as an infant was unbelievable, a lovely baby with rims of fat with sprigs of blonde hair on top of her head. Mama said that the gossip was that I must be "the Milk Man's baby."

Circus people during this time were known to look for certain oddities such as the tallest, shortest, skinniest, fattest, etc. to have on display at the circus. Mama said that someone from the circus came and wanted to show this unusual big fat baby with blonde sprigs of hair on top of her head. However, Mama and Daddy would not hear of it.

Many years later Mama tried to get copies of the only picture that she had of me during this time so she allowed a Traveling Photographer (very common during that time), to take the picture to make copies. She said when he returned with the proofs, changes were requested he took the picture and proof with him and never returned. Mama suffered such consternation over the years about the loss of my baby picture.

It is almost unbelievable that I could have been that big since, I was always petite throughout my life, never at any time weighing more than 130 pounds. During the time I was born, Black people born in Louisiana like other places in the South were classified as "Colored," so I imagine my birth certificate would have listed my race as Colored.

My mother, Josephine Coleman, a black woman was born in Jena, Louisiana in 1905. My mother was the youngest of nine children. Her mother had died giving birth to her so she never really had the opportunity to know her mother and was basically raised by her father and older siblings.

My father, Preston Wilson, was born in Bastrop, Texas, in 1898. He said that he was Choctaw Indian. However, records found recently listed his father as white but did not list the race of his mother. He never talked about the race of his parents. He said he left home at age thirteen. He came to Good Pine, Louisiana sometime in the early twenties following the logging industry where he worked as a lumber grader.

My father was married once prior to being married to my mother. His first wife had died giving birth to their second child, a son Iteamer. At the time of her death, they had a four-year-old daughter, Beatrice. My father kept his daughter Beatrice with him but allowed his wife's sisters, two old school teachers from Little Rock, Arkansas, to take and raise his baby son Iteamer.

When his daughter was four, he married Mama and to that union I was born. Mama was sixteen when they were married, and I was born when she was seventeen years old. So at seventeen Mama was raising both me and Daddy's four-year-old daughter, Beatrice.

Paternal and Maternal Grandparents

I did not know much about my paternal grandparents. I only knew from my father that they were Steve and Effie Wilson who were from Bastrop, Texas. Records found recently showed that Steve Wilson, a white was man born in 1866, to Effie Wilson, born 1870 (no race listed). The record showed that he had four sons, my father Preston (1898), Edward (1895), Jim (1906), Frank (1908), and two sisters, Birdie (1901) and Effie (1904). I never met any of them.

I did know much more about my maternal grandparents, Sylas and Florence Coleman, who were both Black and were from Archie, Louisiana. I know that my maternal grandmother, Florence Coleman, had died in 1905 giving birth to my mother, Josephine. I know that in addition to Mama, my grandparents had other children Lavinia, Lula, Lott, Walter, Union, Rosie, Dennis, Brazzie, and Will.

*My maternal grandfather Sylas Coleman & his clan in the early 1900 in Rural
Louisiana (My mother Josephine is the babe in arm)*

After my grandmother died, my grandfather remarried and
had two children, Jenny Lee and one other daughter. I have been
told that he had to leave the small Louisiana town where they
lived after beating two white men for paying the "wrong" kind of
attention to his last two daughters who were said to be very
beautiful. His family, however, was able to hold on to his land
until he was able to return after some years.

I can't remember meeting my grandfather; however I do recall
speaking to him by telephone at least once when I was around
seven or eight.

I knew more about Mama's sisters and brothers than other
family members. I was very close to her sister Lula and had lived
with her sisters Lula and Jenny Lee for short periods of time. I
particularly remember her brother Uncle Union, because he owned
a grocery store and a theater that I loved going to when we went to
visit Mama's family in Louisiana. I was also fascinated by her brother

Lott because he actually made shoes as well as repaired them. I also remember fondly her sisters Rosie and Lavinia. Many of her siblings migrated to other areas of the country mainly California.

Encountering Separation and Divorce Early in Life

When I was two years old, Mama and Daddy separated, and Mama and I moved to Rochelle, Louisiana near relatives. However, Mama's family thought that she would have a better opportunity for work in Houston, so when I was around three or four years old, Mama and I moved to Houston, Texas.

They say that the events you remember early in life are those that are most traumatic to you. So the first event that I most clearly recall is the move to Houston and leaving my half sister Beatrice behind. I remember that Mama wanted to bring Beatrice with us, but Daddy would not allow it, so there was a lot of crying. Mama had become mother to Beatrice and wanted to raise us together. We had become so attached to each other, so the separation was very traumatic.

After moving to Houston, Mama made many trips back so that I could spend time with Daddy, who I dearly loved. For some reason one of the lasting images still in my mind is the one of me sitting on my Daddy's lap during these visits and looking up at him and saying over and over "Daddy, Daddy. Also seeing and being with my half sister Beatrice and my cousins Barbara and Bubba (Uncle Lott's children) were the highlight of the trip.

However, Beatrice on every trip wanted to come with us. Mama was always begging Daddy to let her come with us and live, but Daddy would have no parts of that. It was so awful each time leaving her behind.

What I Learned

I learned that believing children are more resilient than adults is simply incorrect. Adults like to say when children's lives are disrupted "that children are resilient and they will be ok." They usually say this to make themselves feel better and less guilty.

Since resiliency by definition is the ability to properly adapt to stress and adversity, how would a child have greater coping skills to adapt to stress and adversity than an adult? Children are just forced to tolerate whatever situation they are placed in by adults because they are helpless to do anything about it.

For many who are without a secure foundation, there can be emotional scars from unresolved confusion and fear that can last a lifetime. I could only imagine what my half sister Beatrice must have felt when we left her. First losing her natural mother in death during the birth of her baby brother and now losing her second mother, my mama to separation and divorce.

I was fortunate in that I had a constant source of reassurance from Mama that everything would be all right and I felt safe. Feeling safe and loved is a bigger deal to children than any material provision.

A disruption in a child's life may be the result of many things such as death, divorce, separation, relocation, financial crises, safe harbor, or for better opportunities. Whatever the reason, children need to be reassured constantly that they are loved and will be safe. That worked for me as I faced other separations in life as a child.

Chapter 2

Growth and Change

Mama and I In Houston

Mama and I In Houston

Somewhere between leaving Louisiana and moving to Houston in 1926, Mama met and later married the nicest man, Billy Zeigler. I called him Mr. Billy. He loved me as if I was his own. His family loved me also and made me feel so special. He wanted to adopt me, but Mama would not agree. In later years I found that he had listed me as his daughter anyway, according to the 1930 census.

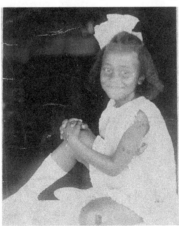

Orlean age 4 or 5

From what I understand, Mr. Billy's sister was always interfering in Mama and Mr. Billy's marriage, so after a few years, Mama left Mr. Billy, and we moved to Fort Worth to live with her sister Lula.

Although I loved Mr. Billy and his family, I was not bothered about leaving as long as I was with Mama because she always made me feel so loved and safe. I can never remember seeing any strife between Mama and Mr. Billy, and perhaps I was too young to see that she was unhappy. I just saw moving to Fort Worth as an adventure because we were going to live somewhere new with Mama's sister and her family.

Life in Fort Worth in the Early 1930s

As far as my first name is concerned, I am known as Orlean, however, I believe that my birth name was Olene. Upon entering elementary school at Gay Street Elementary School in Fort Worth, someone in school administration must have thought that Olene must be a misspell since some were pronouncing it Orlean like the city New Orleans, so she wrote my name as Orlean on all my record, and it became the official spelling of my name since I did not have a birth certificate to prove otherwise. Mama never challenged the change in spelling (which was unusual for Mama).

Living with Aunt Lula the Prima Donna

Mama and I lived with Aunt Lula and her husband, Uncle Ezell, their son, Howard, and daughter, Lucille, for about six months until Mama could work and get our own place. Aunt Lula in her own way was a "prima donna." Whenever she napped during the day because there was no screen on the doors or windows, she would have me swat flies so that they would not annoy or interfere with her "beauty rest."

She offered to pay me one penny for each fly I killed. I gladly took the job because I was always interested in making money even if it was swatting flies. Aunt Lula had the nerve to complain about having to pay me so much because I killed and piled up a lot of flies.

Her daughter, Cousin Lucille and my idol, was a teenager at the time and could care less about making money swatting flies because all she cared about was her secret boyfriend named Marvin. She hid his picture under rocks in the outdoor toilet. I would see her taking the picture out and kissing it, so when I went to use the outdoor toilet, I would also take the picture out and kiss it.

One time, as I reached for the picture, I mistakenly pushed it farther under the rock, and it fell out of reach. When Lucille found out, she was extremely upset with me, but she could not tell anyone because she was not supposed to have a boyfriend in the first place. But she made my life miserable because I had lost her beloved boyfriend's picture. I, on the other hand, could not wait for "Poop" collection day on Daisy Lane in the hopes that I would find the picture when the rocks were moved around the toilet to empty the septic tank....

Once a week the city would come with a horse drawn wagon to haul away the "poop" from Daisy Lane. You never needed to look at a calendar; everyone knew it was Wednesday poop removal day from the awful smell. I was hoping that when they moved the rocks from around the toilet, I would find the picture. However, that didn't happen, so more misery from Lucille.

Aunt Lula's Finishing School

One day I came home from school mimicking a classmate who walked with her toes pointed inward (pigeon-toed). I thought it was cute, so I was practicing how to walk that way, but Aunt Lula saw me and was not at all pleased.

This was the beginning of my training on "how to be a lady." Although Mama instilled good values in me and dressed me well no matter what sacrifice she had to make, it was Aunt Lula who taught me "how to be a lady." I have no idea where Aunt Lula learned all of the social graces because she only completed the fifth grade and never worked outside the home; but she knew. She taught me to speak, sit, and walk "like a lady." She would make me walk with a book on my head so that my posture would be erect. She said sleeping on my stomach would help me have shapely buttock, which would give me a nice figure. To what degree this is true I don't know, however, I was always known to have a "nice figure."

Aunt Lula the
"prima donna"

She always taught me how to take care of my skin and to always use only "Vaseline" on my face and that if I did, I would always have a "smooth complexion." She would remind me to do this up until the end of her life. I took her advice, and it has worked. Thank God they still make Vaseline products.

I enjoyed my early childhood. Actually I have very fond memories growing up as a kid in Fort Worth. The truth is it was the happiest time of my early childhood. I especially enjoyed growing up with my dear friends Rosie and Lawrence who were my neighbors and Papa Leamon's half siblings. We did crazy things like standing on the high front porch and seeing who could pee the farthest. For obvious reasons Lawrence always won. Lawrence would also bury money and try to make us believe he found it. He was my very best friend and confidante.

We were happy kids oblivious to much of the racial prejudices or restrictions that existed. As growing children, we did not even know that Jim Crow laws existed.

> "Jim Crow was the name of the racial caste system that operated primarily, but not exclusively, in southern and border states, between 1877 and the mid-1960s. Jim Crow was more than a series of rigid anti-black laws; it was a way of life. Under Jim Crow, African Americans were relegated to the status of second-class citizens. Jim Crow represented the legitimization of anti-black racism." www.ferris.edu/jimcrow/what.htm

As a child I was not knowingly subjected to racism like older Blacks who had to work outside of the Black community. As children we pretty much stayed in our community, a community where I was treated kind and special. We barely saw whites except for salesmen and occasional the police.

However, there were two areas that really got my attention, even as a child because I had questions that were never quite explained to my childlike understanding. Perhaps the grown-ups in my life were just trying to protect me from having the burden of dealing with the racial and social inequalities of that time.

The first one that got my attention was what happened when we went to the movie theater in town. On Saturday night in Fort Worth, we would go to the movies. Of course, we had to wait until the theater closed for the White patrons. After closing time, they would reopen the theater for the Blacks ("Colored" patrons). We were not allowed to enter through the front cashier's window area. We had to enter through an alleyway.

While waiting Whites, mostly teenager boys would stand on a balcony overlooking the alley way and pour water down on the Black people standing in line waiting to get into the theater and then run away. Either you dodged the water and waited to see the movie or got wet and mad and went home. Lucky for me I was never doused. I didn't understand why these White boys were doing this. I just thought, as most children did, that they were just bad boys, not understanding that their actions had racial implications.

The Second area was related to the annual Juneteenth Celebration. I recall that every year we would all travel to Dallas, Texas for the Juneteenth Celebration, where once a year the "For Whites only" stadium/park in Dallas, Texas would allow Black folk to celebrate Juneteenth. Because I was a child and not aware of the racial overtones, it became a day of fun and celebration. What I didn't understand was why this was the only day Blacks could visit the park.

> Juneteenth marks the anniversary of June 19, 1865; the day that Texas slaves learned they were free. The Emancipation Proclamation, issued by President Abraham Lincoln on January 1, 1863, freed slaves in Confederate states and areas not

under Union control, but the slaves in Texas were not told they were legally free for more than two years."   Encyclopedia 2.thefreeddictionary.com/Juneteenth

What I learned

I learned that most children are oblivious to racial hatred and animosity and obviously learn this from older adults based on their own experiences and encounters.How we explained to children about discrimination based on racial, ethnic, gender, religious, disability and class differences will shape how they handle these prejudices in their adult life and whether or not they will continue the practices themselves.

Some adults pass on their own prejudicial beliefs, animosity, bigotry, and practices because they want to maintain some false sense of superiority or "way of life" which usually is based on fear and ignorance, While others say they want to protect their children from the ills of discrimination, profiling, and brutality.

Even though I would encounter racial animosity in later life that sometimes made me very angry and disappointed and at times even caused me to strike back; however, once the situation was over, I never harbored racial hatred or passed it on to my children. I believe that this was in large part due to how my mother and older adults in my life were able to handle these situations without passing on any deep feelings of racial animus to me.

School life in Fort Worth

After Gay Street Elementary, I enrolled into Crawford Junior High School in Fort Worth, however, during that time, the Crawford Junior High was being renovated, so we were relocated to I.M. Terrell High School for the interim.

Because we were now a part of the high school student body we were allowed to participate in the high school activities such as Homecoming and the Annual Field Day. Each homeroom class was allowed to have a representative to compete for the title of Queen over the festivities.

I am not sure exactly how it happened since I was fairly new to the school, but I was chosen as Homeroom class representative. I was reluctant to run and had to be coaxed by my homeroom teacher to compete. As an eighth grader, I did not give too much thought to winning because it was understood pretty much that the title would be given to a high school girl.

To my surprise, I received the student body's popular vote and was chosen as Queen of the whole school. This was unheard of for an eighth grader, but because I was voted in by the student body, school administrators had to allow it. So, for the first time in the school's history, at least up until this time no one except a high school girl had been chosen as the High School's Homecoming Queen.

Obviously, there was bad feeling from the high school girls who thought that one of them should have been chosen, but none confronted me directly. I was always friendly to everyone and treated them with respect and perhaps it has paid off.

Schools Participate
In Big Field Day;
Wortham Field

Friday, all schools turned out to participate in another Field Day celebration at Wortham Field.

It was another day of joy, frolic and fun to the thousands of schools lined up in formation demonstrating various dance numbers. The schools also competed in track.

The main event of the afternoon was the crowning of Miss Orlena Wilson, I. M. Terrell eighth grade student, as queen. Miss Wilson was chosen queen by popular vote of the I. M. Terrell student body.

Orlean Age 12 or 13 I.M. Terrell
High School Queen 1936

Article from local newspaper on the
Crowning of the Eight Grader as Queen.

One of the most exciting parts of being chosen queen was being awarded a trip to the Historical Black College Prairie View A&M College. What an exciting trip that was for an eighth grader.

Because I was queen, I readily became the girlfriend of the star football player Rufus Nettles (nickname, Blondie). I was told later that he had campaigned on my behalf to win the Queen's title, because he thought that I was cute, shapely, friendly, and "different," whatever that was supposed to mean.

Even though I now was supposed to be Rufus's girlfriend, we never had one date during this time. Mama said I was too young to date and not only that, Rufus was two grades ahead of me. Rufus could only walk me home from school. Well, he couldn't really walk me all the way home; I would only allow him to walk me to my street. Eventually Mama allowed him to walk me to the front door.

I really liked Rufus, but he was much more serious about me, which in later life would seriously impact the direction his life would take.

Although I had many school friends, my friend Janet was special. Like Mama even at the age of twelve or thirteen, I was a natural nurturer, so when I learned that Janet's mother had died suddenly, I felt it was my obligation to try and take care of her. We became very close friends, and we still are to this very day. After some eighty-plus years, we still talk frequently.

Church Life in Fort Worth

Although Mama was not super religious, I always knew that she had an abiding faith in God and taught me to have faith and to know that "God will always be with you." I seemed to sense God's presence always, so I was always eager to know more about God. I was intrigued with how Miss Mack, the elderly women who took care of my friends Rosie and Lawrence after their mother died from childbirth would always seem to be reading her Bible. Although I was later told she did not know how to read. However, there was something about how she recited scripture and talked about God and Jesus that so impressed me as a child.

There was also a Pentecostal church on the corner from where I lived that was a fascination to me and my friends and we would stand outside, watch, and practice mimicking the way they worshipped.

Because my family were all Baptist. I affiliated as a child at Mount Zion Hill Baptist Church. I particularly remember the

Pastor, a Rev. Tally, and how much I enjoyed competing to be the first to find the Bible verses and other scriptures that were called out. Perhaps Miss Mack had something to do with that.

I also enjoyed BYPU (Baptist Young People Union) which you hardly ever hear about today. This was great fun because in addition to learning "Christian principles for living," you got to socialize and meet cute church boys. Whether I was in Church or not I somehow always sensed the presence of God with me and that I had his favor, even though I did not fully understand it.

What I learned

First About School Life:

This was probably the first time in my life that I became acutely aware that people liked you for various reasons, some for superficial reasons such as how you look, dress, your skills or intellect, possession, or how popular you are. While others just like you for the kindness, compassion, and respect you show them. I figured out early that the latter was what was most important.

I learned about competition and the mixed emotions that came with winning, especially when it causes a schism between friends. You wonder whether or not it is worth it all.

I also learned that children must be taught to be compassionate and sensitive and to know that it is okay to befriend other children who may be hurting, different, timid, withdrawn, and friendless. I believe that this would go a long way toward putting an end to bullying. Mama taught me never to gossip or say mean things about other kids.

I have learned however that children need to see their parents or other adults in their lives model compassionate behavior for them. If they see adults not showing compassion or hear adults speaking ill about someone who is different, they will model that behavior you can count on it.

Second about My formative Religious Training:

Having some early foundational religious experience has assisted me in my search in trying to understand my relationship with God. I believe that all children will benefit from some religious foundational training, even if they decide later not to be religious at all. I found that at great times of difficulty and challenges, it was my religious foundation that helped to assure me that there is a God who was greater than my situation.

Chapter 3

Transitioning

A New Daddy

After being a single parent for some time, Mama married for the third and final time to the man who would be her husband for fifty-six years and a father to me for the next sixty-two years of my life; he was Papa Leamon Lockhart. However, I always had my biological father in my life who I always loved very much.

Papa Leamon was five years younger than Mama, so sometimes it felt as if Mama was raising me and Papa Leamon at the same time. Turns out Papa Leamon and Mama ended up being a good team. Together they turned our small "shotgun house" into a café.

> A shotgun house is a narrow rectangular domestic residence, usually no more than twelve feet (3.5 m) wide, with rooms arranged one behind the other and doors at each end of the house. It was the most popular style of house in the Southern United States from the end of the American Civil War (1861–65), through the 1920s. https://en.wikipedia.org/wiki/Shotgun_house.

We stayed in the back two rooms, and we turned the living room or the front room into a café where we sold food and takeout orders.

A Real Cafe

It wasn't long before Mama and Papa Leamon rented a real Café. Around 1935 or '36, Big Harry, a Jewish merchant in town, was retiring and rented us his grocery store with living quarters in the back. We renovated and turned the store section into a real café. It even had an indoor bathroom.

Our café was known for its special hot links, which we grilled outside in a big open pit. Inside we had tables, a dance floor, and a jukebox. I was a good dancer, so I would entertain the patrons. The patrons would love to see me do the "snake hip dance." I would snake all the way down and pat the floor and snake all the way up. The customers just loved it, but Mama wouldn't allow them to tip me for dancing or for serving.

I got good at helping with running the café, especially when it came to keeping up with the money. Even though I was only twelve or thirteen, I was always good at handling money. In addition to running the café, Papa Leamon also sold block ice and worked at a downtown hotel doing cleaning.

Papa Leamon and Mama Leaving Fort Worth

Papa Leamon was always trying to do better so while working at the hotel, he met a white man who was driving cars from Detroit to California and taking loads of people (White People) on the way. He liked Papa Leamon, and when Papa Leamon told him how much he wanted to go to California, he promised that the next time he came through and picked up a load, he could come along and that Papa Leamon would have to pay him twelve dollars.

Well one day in 1937, that man came through, and Papa Leamon excitedly called Mama on the telephone and said, "Jo, get my clothes ready because I have a chance to go to California, and I need to leave right away, and I will send for you once I get there and get settled."

Later Papa Leamon told how on the way to California when they would stop for food he was often refused services because he was Colored and how the group (all whites) would stand up for him telling the restaurant or café owner that unless he could be served, they would all leave.

So according to Papa Leamon they would give him a table way in the back, but at least he could get a hot meal on that long trip to California. Often one of the white riders from the car would sit with him so that he did not have to eat alone.

Upon arriving in California, Papa Leamon was supposed to stay with his good friend who had moved to California sometime earlier, but he and his wife were away working on what was known as a "couples job," which was very common during that time.

Meanwhile, Mama contacted her sister Jenny Lee and her husband to arrange for him to stay with them for *a* while. Papa Leamon went job hunting the very first day however he found that he could only find "couples jobs," which meant that he would need Mama to come to California right away.

As soon as we could make arrangements to close the café, Mama was off to California. Mama closed the café and gave the café equipment to Aunt Lula before leaving for California.

Separated from Mama for the First Time

Mama could not afford to take me at the time. In addition, I was also still in school with a few months left before school was out, so Mama left me with my Aunt Lula and Uncle Ezell. Although

I was with my Aunt Lula, her husband, Uncle Ezell, who I had lived with when we first came to Fort Worth, I have never felt so alone. I cried all Christmas Day that year, which was my birthday. It was the first time Mama had left me, ever, and the first time we had been separated.

What I learned

From this time in my life I learned that when two people work together on one accord, like I saw with Mama and Papa Leamon, that there is nothing that cannot be accomplish even with meager resources.

Next, I learned that allowing children to take on adult responsibility under supervision like Mama and Papa Leamon did when they allowed me to help run the café and trusted me to handle all of the money, that it gave me a sense of self-worth and confidence.

I also learned that twelve and thirteen is the age according to a noted psychologist that a child develops a sense of self and personal identity. So allowing them to take on greater responsibility will give them a sense of fulfillment, a strong sense of self and can shape in a positive way what they will become.

Next, I learned from Papa Leamon's account of his trip to California that there are good people of all races who will stand up for right like the people he traveled with who stood up when he was denied accommodations because he was a Negro or Black.

Chapter 4

Moving to Los Angeles

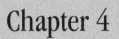

*T*he school year ended for me in December 1937, and it was time for me to join Mama and Papa Leamon in Los Angeles. Everyone, especially "Blondie" and my friend Janet were very upset because I was leaving. Most of my friends thought I was going to Hollywood, and I didn't tell them any better since based on Aunt Lula's tutelage, Hollywood seemed to me where I should be going.

When I arrived in Los Angeles in January 1938 Mama and Papa Leamon we're working as a couple for a wealthy family. Mama also was working as a hotel maid. Papa Leamon had three jobs he usually got home around 2:30 A.M. and had to start all over again early the next morning. While they were away, I stayed with Aunt Jenny Lee, Uncle CD, and their daughters, Dorothy and Gladys. Times were tough and jobs were hard to come by, so at the time neither Aunt Jenny Lee or Uncle CD was currently unemployed.

Mama and Papa Leamom would pay for us to stay there and buy all the food. Because Mama and Papa Leamon worked as a couple and were away during the week, I was often left with my aunt and uncle.

After several months, we left and went to stay in the house of Papa Leamon's friends Ms. Alberta and Mr. Shadrick until Mama found a small one-bedroom duplex to rent.

Although I never asked for it, Mama always wanted me to have the best of everything, so she and Papa Leamon gave me the bedroom to decorate for myself, and she and Papa Leamon slept on the murphy bed (a bed that could be pulled down from the wall) in the living room. To this day I still have a nightstand from that first bedroom I decorated for myself in 1938.

Starting School in an Integrated Setting

In September 1938, I started school at McKinley Junior High school, Los Angeles, which was fully integrated. There were white kids, black kids, Mexican, Japanese, and Chinese kids. Even Dorothy Dandridge the film and theatre actress, singer, and dancer attended school there. I had seen her in Texas as she and her sister danced and sang their way to California.

> Dorothy Dandridge Perhaps best known for being the first African-American actress to be nominated for an Academy Award for Best Actress for her performance in the 1954 film *Carmen Jones*. wikipedia.org.

For me, this was the first integrated school that I had attended, and even though this was a new and different setting for me, I just believed that God was with me and that I would find favor with the students and teachers, and I did. I was very good in math, so the teacher even allowed me to help the other students who were having trouble.

Accompanying First Lady Mrs. Eleanor Roosevelt and Mary McLeod Bethune

Although I had only been at the school for a few months, I again received favor. When the First Lady Mrs. Eleanor Roosevelt came to visit the newly established Federal Nursery School located near the school campus, I was selected by the teachers to accompany her and the renowned Negro educator and activist Mary McLeod Bethune on the tour of the site. I had no idea how I was chosen from among all of the students to escort them except God's favor.

March 17, 1938: First Lady Eleanor Roosevelt visits the Federal Nursery School in the 1000 block of East Vernon Avenue during a tour of government relief activities in Los Angeles. (L.A. Times).

There was also a picture of me with Mrs. Roosevelt and Mrs. McLeod Bethune on the front page of local community newspaper. Which I am now unable to locate.

— The Graduating Class of William McKinley Junior High School, '38 —

Orlean seated first row thirteenth from left.

My school life at McKinley had come to a close and now onward and upward to high school.

What I learned

I have come to understand that how we come onto this planet and to whom, whether we are born into a life of opulence or lack has little to do with our purpose for being here.

Until a child can begin to think for themselves, they are guided by what their parents tell them about who they are and what they will become. Planting negative thoughts could interfere with them discovering their life's purpose.

It is so important for parents to tell children no matter the circumstance of their birth how important and special they are and that they can achieve anything and for the most part a child will believe just that...

As long as I can remember, Mama made me feel good about who I was and what I could do in this world. Therefore, with praise came confidence and an expectancy that people would treat me special, and they did. I was learning to expect God's favor, and his favor I got. I also expected man's favor, and man's favor I received even in times of hardship and pain. The Holy Scripture says that "whatsoever a man thinketh in his heart so is he." He is what he thinks that he is. Good or bad, success or failure.

Mama use to use this little mantra with me and I would repeat: YOU CAN, YOU WILL, AND YOU MUST.

Chapter 5

Adjusting to Life in Los Angeles

*A*lthough I made a lot of friends at my new school, my first and closet friends were Josie and Velma who we called "Sister Girl" from my neighborhood. As a matter of fact, when I first came to California, I had stayed back a semester so that I could start school that September with Josie and Sister Girl, the only persons my age that I knew in Los Angeles at the time. I was one semester grade ahead coming at midterm from Texas, so it just put me on track with where I should have been.

I always told myself that I stayed back because I was one semester grade ahead; however, if the real truth be told, I did not want to go to high school early because I was afraid. Everything in Los Angeles was new and too fast to me. Josie and Sister Girl made me feel safe, so we would go off to high school together.

The first and only time I ditched school ever was with Josie (Josie Bell Reed and Sister Girl (Velma Johnson). Josie and I loved school, but Sister Girl seemed to care less. One day while walking to school, Sister Girl said, "I am not going to school today. I am going back home and make me a pan of enchiladas." I protested, but when I saw Josie following her, I yelled wait for me. We ate enchiladas the whole day.

Josie and Sister Girl were also my church pals. In addition to going to the popular Mount Zion AME Church, what we love most was the small storefront church of Rev. Collins on Hooper

& Forty-Sixth Street where we would help clean and sweep the floors and arrange the chairs for the worship services.

Off to High School and Finding Favor

Well it was time to go to high school and I was going to the popular (Jeff) Jefferson High School. Like McKinley Junior High School, Jefferson High School was fully racially integrated with Blacks, white, Mexicans, Japanese and Chinese.

Although there were other integrated high schools in Los Angeles at the time, Jefferson High was the most popular school in Los Angeles where Blacks attended.

My first Day at Jefferson High School 1939

On my very first day, I met the man who I would eventually fall in love with and marry, Harold Washington. Harold was a senior, very popular, and had the "gift of gab." He was on the committee who welcomed the new freshmen to Jefferson and immediately focused all of his attention toward me. I was shy and really did not know how to handle this attention.

Plus, Rufus (Blondie) from Fort Worth I.M. Terrell "Star Football Player" had talked his folks into letting him come to Los Angeles to live with relatives and finish high school, so he could be close to me, and they allowed him to come. When Harold really tried dating me, I told him that I had a boyfriend who had moved out here from Fort Worth.

Being the silver-tongued city slicker that he was; he befriended Blondie and would make sure he was around when Blondie came to see me.

Blondie caught on to his plot, and he could see that I was falling for Harold, so he graduated from Jeff and, to my knowledge, went back to Fort Worth. He had given up lots to come to Los Angeles, perhaps even a football scholarship.

I regretted it later but at the time I was head over heels in love with Harold Washington and unfortunately, I couldn't see any further than that. I had other suitors during that time but Harold was my "main squeeze."

Harold (1938)　　　*Orlean (1939)*

Finding Favor at Jefferson High

I found favor among my classmates at Jefferson High School, and as they say, I became very popular. I became a part of many school activities. I joined many academic clubs and was elected as Vice President of Student Government.

STUDENT GOVERNMENT
(Pictured below Student Government, Orlean, second from the end on middle row).

Row 1 S. Sanchez, J. Byas, A. Burris, B. Toles, E. Tom, J. Salazar, Row 2 L. Murillo, C. Mayfield, M. Jackson, R. Graham, O. Wilson, M. Mounday, Row 3 G. Lomax, O. King, L. Beavers, R. Cage, C. Nesbit, D. Wylie

I also became a member of several social clubs and made lots of new friends. I was living life the real Jefferson High School way.

Choosing Best Friends and Having Lots of Fun in Los Angeles

During my teenage and young adult life in Los Angeles, there were three people who became my very best friends. Cornelius Marshall (Bud) my best male friend, Josie Bell Reed was my best girlfriend and pal, and Shizuye Wada, a dear school friend. Cornelius Marshall (Bud) was considered as very handsome, and during that time good-looking or "pretty boys" were not known to be tough, but Bud was tough, and nobody and I mean nobody messed with Bud. I believe that he was known to fight often, so he was sent to what now may be called an Alternative School. However, you could not find a more respectful young man. Bud was also from a very prominent Los Angeles family.

My Best male friend Bud 1940   *Orlean & Bud 1939 or '40*

Bud was a real gentleman to me. We did everything together and we really enjoyed the LA scene as teenagers together.

Left to right: Orlean, Bud, Josie, Ted, and Menyon doing the Jabba Walk, a popular dance at the time (1939 or 1940) East Los Angeles Lincoln Park

For some reason I was blind to whether Bud had any affection toward me, although others may not have been. He knew I was Harold's girl, so he maintained his role as my best male friend. I knew that he was always very protective of me especially where Harold was concerned. If he could help it, he would never leave me alone with Harold. Mama trusted Harold with me, but Bud didn't.

When it was prom time, Harold was my date. I am not sure how it happened, but Bud was right there in his tux and went with me and Harold to the prom. I was so naïve, I thought it was fun to have two escorts, and we all have a great time at the prom.

I danced with them both. We went to the "After Prom night" together, and when it was time to go home, Bud was right there and stayed in the car and waited until Harold walked me to the door of my house. Bud did not trust Harold with me, and Harold knew it. Harold pretended that Bud was his friend, and he knew not to make a fuss about Bud going with us *because* Bud didn't take "no stuff" from anybody, and he was always looking out for me.

In later years when Harold and I were getting married Bud finally started dating someone seriously. and eventually married and became a successful Realtor in Los Angeles.

> **Caveat:** (Bud still remained in our lives. When Harold and I had our first child, Ronnie, Bud, who continued to work in his family's barbering business would cut Ronnie's hair and always gave Ronnie lots of attention. I overheard a loud argument between he and Harold about not buying me the house that they both had agreed that I should have and that Bud had agreed to go in with Harold to buy a home for me; Bud was always looking out for me).

Zoot Suit Fad

My best girlfriend Josie was one of my first friends in Los Angeles; as I mentioned earlier, we were also neighbors. We were considered "nice girls," but we knew how to have lots of fun and how to be "Los Angeles fashionable." We were into all of the latest fads like the lady's *version* of the zoot suit.

Orlean in zoot suit (1939)

The zoot suit was originally associated with Afro-American musicians and their sub-culture. Later Chicano and Italians. Anti-Mexican youth riots in Los Angeles during World War II are known as the Zoot Suit Riots. In time, zoot suits were prohibited for the duration of the war, ostensibly because they used too much cloth.[Wikipedia 2014].

Harold and Orlean in Zoot suits—1939

Josie and I would even dress up in riding gear, ladies riding breeches or jodhpurs. We would even carry the crop or whip as if we owed horses. There wasn't a horse in sight. Matter of fact, at that time we didn't even know anyone who owed a horse. It was a fad, and we were just copying what the rich did in the movies.

We would take the bus in our expensive riding gear to downtown Los Angeles and all the people would be staring at us as if we were either insane, rich, owned horses, or in the movies.

Later we did go horseback riding in Artesia, an area farther south of Los Angeles. However, we did not wear those expensive riding duds because we didn't want them spoiled. Whether that made sense, we didn't care because we were into the fashion associated with horseback riding as opposed to actual riding.

One day when we were all dressed in our riding duds, we went to see Mama who worked as a maid in one of the exclusive hotels downtown. When we got there because we were Negro, the doorman made us enter from the back of the hotel. Mama was furious and went and hopped all over that poor doorman and told him he better not ever have her child go through a backdoor. He apologized to me and Josie. Mama was someone to contend with.

In later life when I got married, Josie was my maid of honor, and when she was married, I was her maid of honor.

Orlean as Josie's Maid of Honor   *Josie as Orlean's maid of honor*

Josie and I remained friends as adults and continued to live in the same neighborhood as adults for many years.

Losing my Friend Shizuye to Japanese Internment Camp

One of my dearest school friends at Jefferson High School was Shizuye Wada. She was so outgoing with a lot of personality. I use to describe

her personality as "Jazzy." Although I had many Japanese classmates Shizuye was the most outgoing and we were such great friends. She even gave me a friendship ring.

Shizuye Wada 1941

It was the spring of 1941, and we were graduating, and all of us were getting formal dresses for the graduation exercise. I can't recall just why we were not going to wear the usual cap and gown, but the girls were to wear formal gowns and the boys dark dress suits. This would be the first time that caps and gowns would not be worn.

As a matter of fact, I had designed my graduation formal gown myself and promised Mama if she would have it made to order for me that whenever I got married, I would wear it as my wedding dress and I did.

Everyone was so excited about our impending graduation, which was scheduled for June 1941. But our excitement was horribly quashed by the news that all of our Japanese Classmates and their families were being sent to Japanese Internment or War Camps. They would lose their homes, businesses and all of their assets. The whole school was in tears including all of the teachers. Our Class was especially hurt because it was graduation time.

Even though the ceremony was held I can't seem to recall if the Japanese students were able to graduate. It turned out to be an awful time. How could this happen? We couldn't understand it. We were later told that this had happened because even though they were citizens of the United States their loyalty to Japan was questionable.

According to historians many Americans worried that citizens of Japanese ancestry would act as spies or saboteurs for the Japanese government. Fear—not evidence—drove the US to place over 127,000 Japanese-Americans in concentration camps for the duration of WWII. Over 127,000 United States citizens were imprisoned during World War II. Their crime? Being of Japanese ancestry. Despite the lack of any concrete evidence, Japanese Americans were suspected of remaining loyal to their ancestral land. Anti-Japanese Paranoia increased because of a large Japanese presence on the West Coast. In the event of a Japanese invasion of the American mainland, Japanese Americans were feared as a security risk. Succumbing to bad advice and popular opinion,

President Roosevelt signed an executive order in February 1942 ordering the Relocation of all Americans of Japanese ancestry to Concentration Camps in the interior of the United States. Evacuation orders were posted in Japanese-American communities giving instructions on how to comply with the executive order.

(UShistory.org/us/51e.asp)

I have no idea what ever happened to my friend Shizuye, since there was no way to communicate with her. I have thought of her often over the years, and I will never forget her.

I am almost sure that the people who wanted the Japanese interned did not have good Japanese neighbors or classmates or friends like Shizuye. It is easy to fear and hate what you don't know.

What I learned

You may get to know many people during your life. but when the sifting is over, there are only a very few who you will want to keep as your real or best friends even when you are young. I believe that there are kindred spirits and that they seek out each other. Although I had many friends there were only three that I considered as my best friends.

During this tremendous period in my life, I learned that "youth" is not wasted on the young as I have heard said. Youthful spirits are pioneering spirits. It is easy to see why all of the important changes is this world have been started by youth movements. For the most part the young are fearless and do not see limitations until someone, usually an older person, whose dreams have been dwarfed or thwarted, tell them what is not possible to do.

My high school years were the most fun free years of my life because my fresh optimism had not yet been doused by troubled waters or negative events. Even when awful things happened, such as when your friend is taken away to an internment camp, somehow you believe that you have the power to right these kinds of wrongs.

I was very moved about all of the injustices that I saw and wanted to do something about it, so right after high school, I went to work for the American Anti-Prejudice Society.

Cementing My Moral Character as a Young Adult

My best memories are the special morning talks with my mother. Mama would wake me up early each morning to have our morning talks before she left for work. Most of these talks were about what needed to done for the day, having good value, how I was always to handle myself as a lady, and above all, having God in my life. I loved these talks so much that I started getting up before Mama and making her a cup of coffee so that we could have "our talk."

My Integrity Tested

My friend Ida and I found out that Bullocks Department Store in downtown Los Angeles were hiring elevator attendants. To land a job at Bullock's would be a prize.

Bullock's was built in 1929 as a luxury department store. The department store served the upper crust of Los Angeles Society. In its heyday, Bullocks Wilshire patrons included Mae West, John Wayne, Marlene Dietrich, Alfred Hitchcock, Greta Garbo, ZaSu Pitts, Walt Disney, and Clark Gable. While struggling to become an actress, a teenaged Angela Lansbury worked as a sales clerk. Future First Lady Patricia Nixon also served a stint on the floor. (en.wikipedia.org/wiki/Bullocks_Wilshire)

I thought that if I could land this job, I would not only get to meet real movie stars, but I would have a chance to be around all of those beautiful clothes I loved so much. Well, we both, Ida and I, landed an interview. We dressed ourselves to "the nines" and went for the interview. We told everyone we knew that we had an interview at Bullocks, and they were all excited. We could just see ourselves in those sharp uniforms elevator women wore. However, when the interviews were over, I was hired and Ida wasn't. I could not understand it because Ida was so beautiful with such lovely hair and great personality. We both cried all the way home. Later that day we found out that Bullock's was only hiring light-skinned Negroes for the Elevator Attendant job, and Ida was not a light-skinned Negro. I was so angry and vowed that if Ida's skin color was not good enough to be an Elevator Attendant, and then my skin color was not good enough. I turned down the job. Everyone could not believe that I was turning down the job since a job like that was hard to come by in 1940. Mama said she was so proud of me standing up for what was right. She was especially proud since she knew how much I wanted that job.

What I learned

Standing up for another person or for what is right sometimes costs short-term, but it builds character in the long run. It's easy to speak up when it costs you nothing, but correspondently the reward is nothing.

There was no better lesson to get me on my road to standing up for others and fighting injustices than standing up as a young person for my friend Ida even if it meant not having that ideal job at Bullocks Wilshire and meeting all of those movie stars and being around all of those beautiful clothes, which I always loved.

Chapter 6

Finding My Way

After High School

I was always concerned about discrimination and injustices of all kinds, though there was less of it in Los Angeles, but it still existed. After high school I went to work as a secretary for the American Anti-Prejudice Society headed by the Rev. C.T. Tucker. The American Anti-Prejudice Society has been a California Corporation since March 23, 1940. I worked for the organization while I attended Los Angeles City College.

Sometimes later I also landed a job with an exclusive Jewish Millinery manufacturer in downtown Los Angeles where the owner really loved me. I learned to make hats, which I had a real flare for. She also allowed me to do all of the banking. That was saying something considering that I was only eighteen and Negro. I was always good at handling money, and the owner could see that.

I could also see that she had plans for my future and was extremely upset when I told her that I was getting married to the love of my life, Harold Washington. She tried her best to talk me out of it and even told Mama I was just too young to be getting married, and of course, Mama agreed.

Mama wanted me to not get married so young and continue my education. However, for once in my life I did not even listen to Mama. I even told her that she did not understand anything about being in love. Words Mama had the occasion to remind me of later.

All I knew is that World War II was raging, and Harold, after completing special training as a navigator, was inducted as a Sergeant into the US Army Air Corp. He was sent to Tuskegee to be a navigator with the now-famed Tuskegee Airmen.

"Tuskegee Airmen" refers to all who were involved in the so-called "Tuskegee Experiment," the Army Air Corps program to train African Americans to fly and maintain combat aircraft. The Tuskegee Airmen included pilots, navigators, bombardiers, maintenance, and support staff, instructors, and all the personnel who kept the planes in the air. *www.nps.gov/.../tuskegee/airoverview.htm).*

Once Harold was gone, we kept in touch through letter writing and sending pictures to each other and talked of marriage.

Picture sent to Harold in Tuskegee before we married.
(The picture was entered by the photographer into a contest in San Francisco and won First Prize).

In spite of all the objections, I could think of nothing but marrying Harold, and I did exactly that. On December 23, 1941 two days before my nineteenth birthday, Harold and I were married in a modest home wedding. Mama and I decorated the house and our musician neighbor, Ethel Stewart, rolled over her piano and provided the music. The house and yard were just filled with people—those we invited and those who just heard that Harold and Orlean were getting married and just invited themselves.

The local Negro newspaper The California *Eagle* carried the story and a picture of the ceremony. December 23, 1941

Miss Orlean G. Wilson Bride of Sgt. Washington In Home Ceremony

The California Eagle Newspaper. December 23, 1941.

After the wedding, Harold returned to Tuskegee, and I was asked to return to work at the American Anti-Prejudice Society to head a national membership drive. However, as soon as Harold could arrange it, he sent for me to visit him in Tuskegee.

What I learned

I learned that when two people are in love and they truly want to be married and they are of legal age to be married and nothing will stop them. The best you can do is to have them seek counseling.I strongly believe that there should be a mandatory course in high school on how and when to marry.

I later learned that nineteen was too young to be married, even though it was not uncommon during the '40s for people to be married young, especially during war time. However, Mama and my boss from the Millinery store were right. Hindsight is 20/20.

Chapter 7

Traveling With "Jim Crow"

*I*n every letter I received from Harold, he was saying that any day he might be sent off to the war. As soon as I could, I packed and was off to Tuskegee.

At the famous Los Angeles Union Station, which was opened in 1939 and the filming location for many movies, I met up as planned with Helen Hamilton, who had been recently wedded to Chico Hamilton, who later became a famous American jazz drummer and bandleader. Helen and I had planned to travel together. She was going to be with Chico, who was stationed at some base down south and would be taking the train with me as far as New Orleans. This was just great, which meant that I would have company most of the way to Tuskegee. We both were scared about traveling this far alone.

There were a lot of soldiers on the train, and Mama, Papa Leamon, and Helen's parents seemed concerned and had asked an elderly gentleman passenger named Mr. Walter to look after us girls, and with good reason because the GIs on board were acting scandalous. All kind of unmentionable things were going on, and Mr. Walter hovered over us like a "Mother Hen."

All Negros because of the Jim Crow laws had to ride in the "Colored Car." All railway companies were required to provide separate but equal accommodations for white and colored passengers. Penalty to do so resulted in the passengers or conductors receiving a fine *.en.wikipedia.org/.List_of_Jim_Crow_law_examples*

From the 1880s into the 1960s, a majority of American states enforced segregation through "Jim Crow" laws (so called after a black character in minstrel shows). From Delaware to California, and from North Dakota to Texas, many states (and cities too) could impose legal punishments on people for consorting with members of another race. The most common types of laws forbade intermarriage and ordered business owners and public institutions to keep their black and white clientele separated. (*en.wikipedia.org*)

Mama had tried her best to prepare me for what I would encounter in my travel. She had told me to try to find the "Colored only" accommodation when I had to use the restroom.

When the train reached EL Paso, Texas we were able to get off. Helen and I went off looking for the "colored" restrooms but were unable to find one. No longer able to wait to use a bathroom we went into the "For White Only."

There we found a Mexican woman cleaning the restroom. Helen went in first, and she said nothing. Helen was lighter skinned than me and had a kind of blondish crinkly hair and the woman was unable to tell what race she was. However, when I went in, she came and opened the door on me and said "niggers get out." She was yelling in my face, so "The Josephine" (named after Mama when she became furious) rose up in me and I slapped that women so hard my hand ached. Then Helen and I took off running as fast as we could to the train. Good we did because we had stayed so long looking for that "colored restroom" until the train was pulling off.

I have never been so frightened. There was Mr. Walter outside on the platform nervously pacing up and down when we reached him two soldiers pulled us aboard followed by Mr.

Walter. Once in my seat I could only think what would have happened if we had missed that train. I could just see myself floating down the Rio Grande.

I think I was shocked that a Mexican woman would say those kind of offensive words to me since Mexicans were also subjected to the same kind of Jim Crow laws. Not only that, but many of my neighbors and friends in LA were also Mexican, and race was never an issue. Chinese and Japanese were also subjected to these discriminatory laws depending on what part of the country you were in. Below are Jim Crow signs like the ones I saw were posted throughout public places all over the southwest and deep south.

www.ferris.edu/jimcrow
en.wikipedia.org/wiki/Jim_Crow_laws www.ferris.edu/jimcrow

Mr. Walter got off the train in Houston and left Helen and me in the care of two nice soldiers. They did look out for us and kept the more scandalous GIs away from us. We had a long layover in New Orleans, so the two soldiers who were looking after us went into town in New Orleans to party and left their bags with us. When the train was ready to leave, they were not back, so we had to leave their belongings at the station. We felt really bad about that, but there was nothing else we could do.

This was also the station were Helen and I would part. She took a train to Chico's military base, and I took the one to Birmingham, Alabama where Harold was to pick me up. Boy, that was such a long and lonely ride. I just kept thinking what Mama always told me "God would never leave me alone."

Arriving in Birmingham

Harold was waiting for me when the train arrived in Birmingham, Alabama. After we got my bags and were in the car, we started kissing and lo and behold there was a policeman knocking on the window.

He asked Harold to get out of the car. I heard Harold say, "She's colored" and the policeman let him get back into the car. I asked what that was all about, and Harold told me that he thought I was white. I said he must not have been able to see too well especially my hair, and we laughed so hard.

Harold said that they were cracking down on the GIs at Tuskegee because some of them were bringing their white girlfriends mostly from California to Tuskegee and that it was creating a problem because "race mixing" was not allowed.

Tuskegee, Alabama

We arrived at Tuskegee where the Airmen were training. The Tuskegee Airmen were subjected to racial discrimination, both within and outside the Army. All black military pilots who trained in the United States included five Haitians from the Haitian Air Force, trained at Moton Field and Tuskegee Army Air Field, located near Tuskegee, Alabama. *en.wikipedia.org/wiki/TuskegeeAirmen*

Harold had arranged for me to stay with a woman friend of Booker T. Washington who was the famous African American educator, author, orator, and advisor to presidents of the United States. Between 1890 and 1915, Washington was the dominant leader in the African American community and founder of Tuskegee Institute. *en.wikipedia.org/wiki/BookerT.Washington, ww.biography.com/people/booker-t-washington-*

There were also two other girls from California staying at the same house. One of whom I had attended school with at Jefferson High School in Los Angeles. It was great being there. I loved going to First Call Reveille each morning, listening to the official bugle call would send chills through me.

Jim Crow Up Close and Personal

One morning I went into the town of Tuskegee to get milk and return the empty bottles back in exchange. As I was walking down the sidewalk, I saw Black people of all ages get off and back on the sidewalk at various intervals, and I did not know why. Then I came upon two white girls about my age, and they yelled, "Nigger don't you know that you are supposed to get off this sidewalk until we pass?" I saw stars of all colors and "the Josephine" came out in me. I took one of the milk bottles and broke it on the sidewalk so that I could use the jagged edge as a weapon, something I had seen street fighters back in Los Angeles do. As I started toward the girls, they ran. I am not sure if I would have really hurt them, but I wanted them to think I would.

The incident was reported to Base Authority and when Harold came home that evening he told me that he had been called in by his Commanding Officer and told that I was not to ever go back into town. That was fine with me because it did not prevent me from going other places.

When my homeboys from Los Angeles, who were officers in the Airman Corp did not have a date to accompany them to various ceremonies at the officer's club, Harold would allow them to take me. This meant that I was there for most of all of the special ceremonies and to see the various dignitaries who came down from Washington, DC and elsewhere to observe the Tuskegee project firsthand. I still found favor.

What I learned

I learned three important lessons during this period

1. The difference between direct discrimination and group discrimination.
2. The impact of insult on the human spirit.
3. Favor.

For the first time in my life I had come face-to-face with "Jim Crow" on a personal level, and I was ill-equipped to handle it. As a child in Texas, I was aware that racial discrimination existed but never had to personally deal with it. Even in California I was aware of discrimination, but it was more subtle. I had never had to deal with it on such a personal level where I felt it necessary to respond in an aggressive way. I learned that when it is very personal, it elicits all kinds of emotions.

Because God created the human spirit in his own perfect image and likeness, when the human spirit is demeaned, dehumanized, belittled it rings contrary to its greatness, and it will respond in some way in defense of that treatment when it can, and when it can't, there it will likely be pent up anger, hatred, and resentment. Can you image how the elderly Black men who had to move off the sidewalk to let even white children pass must have felt?

I was lucky because I could respond in some way like fighting back and thus did not need to harbor anger, hatred, or resentment. However, had I been a Black male, the results would have more than likely had dire consequences, especially during this time of "Jim Crow." For generations Black men have had to suffer human indignities without being able to respond or even speak out. This has caused pent-up anger, which has been passed down for generations, causing the "Angry Black Male" characterization we hear being used today.

In spite of my restriction, I still received God's favor.

Chapter 8

Back Home to LA:
Joy and Tragedy

Ronnie's Birth

It was not very long after returning home to Los Angeles that I discovered that I was pregnant with my first son, Ronnie. I was so sick the whole time and could not work. Thanks to Harold's Army allotment and Mama and Papa Leamon, I was well taken care of. Harold could not get leave for Ronnie's birth, so Mama and Papa Leamon and Harold's Mother Miss Hazel was there for the joyous birth.

Seeking Employment

When I was able to start work again, I was fortunate to land a job at the historical Lerners Department Store. Jobs were hard to come by during the war (WW II) so I was grateful to get a job, even it meant being a dishwasher. I just wanted to get a foothold in the door because I just knew that I would be blessed and perhaps even find favor.

Although I never actually heard anyone say so, however in my mind I could just hear the talk around town that. "Miss Fashion, "Goodie Two Shoes," and Miss Popularity from Jefferson High School, Orlean Wilson is washing dishes at Lerners. Even Mama asked why I was washing dishes. However, I kept my head high, and I washed those dishes with such a flare that you would have thought that they were made of gold or at the least fine porcelain, and I wore my beige, heavily starched uniform with its white Peter Pan collar as if it was the latest fashion.

Breaking the So-Called "Color Barrier"

The manager of Lerners, a rough-acting Italian from New York, took noticed, and he asked me one day, "Why are you washing dishes? I would like to see you after work." I had no idea why he wanted to see me and felt intimidated about seeing him, thinking I had done something wrong.

When I met with him, he asked me what kind of experience I had. I told him that I had cashiering and handling money at the Millinery shop and in our own café business back in Fort Worth. He told me to come in for work the next day prepared to be a cashier. Nothing but God's Favor.

Even though I had lots of experience handling money, I just knew that I would never be allowed to fill the open cashier's position at Lerners. There were absolutely no blacks working in any positions like this on Broadway in Los Angeles during this time unless they were "Passing for white," which many did, mostly for survival reasons just trying to provide for their family.

I had two thoughts, what would those people who might have talked about my being a dishwasher say now and next, how would all of the white sales women react to the news, since I would be the only Negro cashier the store had ever had.

Rocky Roads Ahead

Well, it wasn't long before I found out how the White Sales Women felt. They hated it as well as did the customers. They all set out to make my life miserable. The sales ladies, mostly Jewish, who worked on a commission basis would take the merchandised and slap it down hard in front of me to ring up.

I would continue to speak to them with respect and cheerfully greet them each day, but they would never respond.

Once a white customer was so angry that she had to pay a Negro for her merchandise that she took the bag dumped it on the floor and walked out. I never lost my composure or said anything in response. The manager knew of what was happening, and he would just knock on the counter and say "keep going." He never once moved me from this position. As a matter of fact, he complimented me on my work. I stayed in this position until I was ready to leave and on my own terms.

What I learned

I learned what most Blacks during this time realized, which was not to internalize or take to heart the results of someone else's fear and ignorance. Because it can cause pent-up anger, hatred, and resentment.

I agree with the statement that what others think of you is not your business. Your business is to always understand and know your own worth.

So, each morning I would do what Mama suggested, which was to cheerfully greet all those women who hated me for my race and treat them with respect. It paid off.

On the Home Front: Tragedy at Miss Hazel
MISS HAZEL

Miss Hazel, Harold's mother, had virtually raised Harold alone, and they were joined at the hip, so to speak. She had married again when Harold was in his late teens, so Harold did have a stepfather. Miss Hazel was a popular beautician and had a beauty shop on Central Avenue. In later years, she and her husband had purchased a large house and like other blacks who had large houses or extra rooms, she would at times rent rooms to GIs who were on leave and had no place to stay. Even in California in the '40s

They could not stay in white hotels. At that time the only black hotel was the Dunbar Hotel. Because of the rich history of the Dunbar Hotel, it is worth mentioning here.

The Dunbar, formerly the Somerville, was built in 1928 by John and Vada Somerville, socially and politically prominent black Angelenos. John Somerville was the first black to graduate from the University of Southern California. The hotel was built entirely by black contractors, laborers, and craftsmen and financed by black community members. For many years, the Somerville was the only major hotel in Los Angeles that welcomed blacks, and it quickly became the place to stay for visiting black dignitaries. https://en.wikipedia.org/wiki/Dunbar _Hotel

In 1928, the Somerville housed delegates to the first NAACP convention held in the western United States. It also hosted prominent African Americans traveling to Los Angeles, including Duke Ellington, Joe Louis, Louis Armstrong, Lena Horne, Paul Robeson, Marian Anderson, and Josephine Baker. It was located on Los Angeles's Central Ave, which was the hub for black-owned businesses or those businesses catering to Blacks. https://en.wikipedia.org/wiki/Dunbar_Hotel

Even though Black GIs could stay at the Dunbar Hotel, most GIs could not afford it on their meager Army allotment. So some stayed at Miss Hazel's and many hung around creating a party-like atmosphere all the time.

Harold was back home from the Army; he was discharged in 1945, and we had moved together in Mama's back house, which I had nicely decorated. He appeared to be adjusting pretty well to being a husband and proud new father to Baby Ronnie. Then tragedy struck.

One evening when I had come from work Harold, ask me to go to a boxing match at The Olympic Auditorium with his mother and stepfather. The Olympic Auditorium was the place in LA for boxing every Tuesday night. It had been built specifically for the 1932 Olympic Games, eventually. The Olympic had weekly boxing shows during the '30s and '40s and is still in existence to this day. *boxrec.com/media/index.php/ Olympic_Auditorium*

I was not in the mood to go to a boxing match. I was tired from working and just wanted to rest. Well, it seems that since I didn't want to go, I guess Harold changed his mind about going as well as his mother and stepfather. While Miss Hazel and others were sitting at the table playing cards with some GIs, a jealous husband whose wife had been frequenting the house came and shot up the place. A bullet hit Miss Hazel and killed her instantly.

Harold went out of his mind and could not be consoled. He blamed everyone for his mother's death, especially me. He said that only if I had agreed to go to the boxing match, Miss Hazel would not have been home, and she would not be dead. Of course, I knew that this was not true, but it still cut very deeply.

After the death of Miss Hazel, Harold was a changed man and started running around. I guess he was trying to soothe his deep hurt. At any rate, it was a devastating blow to me. He was always a woman's man and very popular, so that didn't help any; it just fueled the problem.

Well, we would go back and forth trying to make the marriage work. At one point after his mother's death, we moved into her house, and Harold later sold the house, and we bought our first home together. He seemed to be settling down, so along came my only daughter, Carolyn Jo. I now had just what I always wanted a boy and now a girl.

Chapter 9

Social and Charitable Consciousness

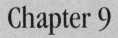

*T*hings went well for a while with Harold and I, and we both involved ourselves in the Social life in Los Angeles. Harold was a member of the popular "Sir Dubuteers," an all-men Social Club who would have many social events.

The Sir Dubuteers Harold's Social Club
Around 1949

The Cooperettes, Inc.-Social and Charitable Consciousness

I later formed a group for social and charitable purposes called the Cooperettes." Although I was plenty social, I was just not interested in belonging to a social group just for the sake of being social. I wanted to belong to a group with a valuable humanitarian purpose.

While reading the paper one day in 1950, I read about a group on the East Coast who had adopted a neighborhood group of trouble teens and was really making a difference in their lives. So, I decided that that was exactly what I wanted to do. So, I pulled together a group of housewives, civil services workers, and other private industry workers. The goal first was to create good fellowship among the members and work as a group for charity.

Although the primary goal was to focus on youngsters in the community including our own but also assist families needing assistance in a way that was most fitting and proper.

Founding members of the Cooperettes. (1950) Orlean is fourth, from right to left

We started out small, and in the first year, we managed to aid needed families with cash and food baskets—not only during the holidays but at any time during the year when we were made aware of a community member in need of help. We also sponsored underprivileged girls for Summer Camp and also served as chaperones for the camp. In addition, we made cash contributions to the Community Chest, The Home for Crippled Children, the local Orphanage, and the Junior Blind.

By 1952 we had identified a community facility we wanted to help. It was the Henry Armstrong Youth Foundation for Delinquent Youth, and we selected this organization as our primary project.

Fundraising for Our Charitable Project

We knew by this time that if we wanted to make a substantial contribution, we would have to do some serious fundraising. Therefore, we had many fundraising events such as the yearly Cabaret shows and several big productions. We hired choreographers and other dance teachers to prepare us for our dance numbers so we would look like professionals.

Our Club member Dance Group at a fund raiser (1955) Orlean first left on front row.

Orlean (left) performing at Fund Raiser (1955)

In addition to the proceeds from the Cabaret that went primarily to support the Center for Delinquent Boys, we would hold dances where the admission was a can of fruit or vegetable juice, which we personally delivered to the Long Beach Tuberculosis Hospital.

Orlean Washington (Seated front Center) Founder of The Cooperettes, Inc. at Formal Dance 1952

Our club became so popular and attracted many new members who were more interested in the social events than in the original purpose. So after a few years, I became disenchanted because the whole purpose for the organization was being missed, so I left the organization.

What I learned

I have learned that when you want to "do good" you find a way. As a group the Cooperettes wanted to help needed families and delinquent youth, and we found a way to raise the resources needed to accomplish this goal. We used a popular forum and hosted gala events such as cabarets. Today however there are so many more creative ways to raise funds for worthy causes.

It is amazing what you can do when you want to help others because "where there is a will there is a way."I learned also that life is about having a purpose and by that time in my life I had come to believe that my purpose was about helping people and not just socializing. So, when the purpose for forming the group was being compromised by those who just wanted to be part of the group because of its popularity, it was time for me to separate myself, which I did.

I also learned that whatever your life's purpose is, you should not allow it to become comprised or maligned. For perhaps, it is your reason for being.

Chapter 10

Having to Move On

*J*ust when I thought my marriage was on track Harold got restless again and felt as if he couldn't commit to anything even his marriage. I believed that he still had unresolved issues related to his mother's death, so I left no stone unturned in trying my best to make my marriage work, but nothing changed.

I was devastated just thinking how I didn't want to lose Harold. Mama and Papa Leamon were always there to comfort me. Mama had to give me many "straight talks" to help me pull myself together because I was falling apart.

I finally realized my rationalizing Harold's behavior was not helping me or the children, so after so much of this back-and-forth, I got the strength to finally get a divorce, so Harold and I were divorced in 1950.

Harold was a brilliant man and an entrepreneur at an early age. As a matter of fact, he owned the first car wash in South Central in his late teens and dabbled in various businesses over the years. In later years he went on to make a real contribution to the community as a real estate developer and was socially and politically involved in Los Angeles.

What I learned

I learned that when you have children, you tolerate more, with the hope that the marriage can be salvaged. Children must take priority in any decision to separate and divorce.

When children say they did not ask to be born, they have a point. I learned that children suffer immensely when there is a divorce, and it should definitely be an action of last resort unless, of course, there is physical or verbal-emotional abuse.

My oldest son tells me to this day how he was affected by my divorce from his father. He relates that how at five, he remembers me crying and being upset and him wanting to protect me. Although I was never abused in any way the instability in the marriage was often the bases for my tears.

We often hear that children are better with one parent in peace than two where there is strife. Where's the proof in other words "where's the beef." I have not necessarily seen this in my ninety-six years of living. Barring violence, either physical or emotional, every effort should be made to keep the family together when at all possible.

Sexual Harassment on the Job

Realizing that I needed to have greater income now as a single parent, when the opportunity came, I left my cashier position at Lerners and took a job in the accounting department at Nate Diamond, a very popular furniture store in Los Angeles. It seemed that Nate gave credit to everyone in South Los Angeles.

When the delivery men would come—and they were all black—I would have to go out to the dock for signatures. The guys were very respectful to me but would compliment me on my appearance. I was always a fashionable but conservative dresser and like most women I knew during this time, I was also "thin and shapely."

I noticed that my boss would touch other women in the office in a disrespectful manner, and they were too afraid to say anything, but he never did this to me. However, one day he came to the dock where I was getting a signature for a delivery and saw how the men admired me, so he decided to take liberty with me to show them that he was my boss, so he touched me on my "behind" in front of them. The "Josephine" came out in full force, and I swung around and slapped my boss as hard as I could. I then went to my desk took my purse and clocked out, knowing I would definitely be fired.

Even though I was a single parent at that time and needed my job, I just was not about to let him disrespect me that way. I knew that God would take care of me and somehow give me the favor I was always expecting.

Believe it or not, after a few days, I was called back to work by the owner, and he apologized to me over and over and asked me to please come back and I did. I never had another problem. He even stopped being disrespectful to the other women in the office.

What I learned

Women have always been subjected to sexual harassment, except during the late '40s and '50s there were no laws or protection against sexual harassment and men were not subject to any consequences for their actions. Women had to mete out their own justice like I did.

I am not saying that women during that time should have gone around slapping their boss like I did, because there are consequences for that as well, such as losing your job.

However sometimes you have to take a stand, even if it means losing your job. Fortunately for me I had been raised by a mother who taught me not to tolerate disrespect from anyone even if it cost.

Had I not taken a stand, I would have been subjected to that disrespectful treatment on an ongoing basis. After I stood up for myself, I not only received multiple apologies from the owner and was asked to return to work, but I was treated with the upmost respect for the rest of the time I was employed there. Believe me, I am not unsympathetic to the fact that many women who were the breadwinner and needed a job had to endure this maltreatment during this time, however, thank God that there are avenues for redress these days and women do not have to tolerate this type of disrespect in order to hold a job.

It was not long after this incident that I was able to secure a position first, as a clerk and later as Head Time Keeper for the City of Los Angeles Refuse Department.

Being Head Timer Keeper meant that I would also have to come to work at 5:00 A.M. during special times to check the trucks and workers out for duty.

There were more than twenty trucks and at least forty men. These men were so respectful and protective of me. Without my asking, two of them would follow behind me as I went along to ensure my safety. I once heard them tell men who had come too close to me for whatever purpose "Don't go any further." They also did other nice and thoughtful things for me. I stayed in this position for eleven and a half years and left to work on a community project called Unity.

Chapter 11

Taking the Marriage Plunge Again

While I was still employed at the City of Los Angeles, I started to date again. I vowed that I would not be serious about anyone in Los Angeles. I didn't want anyone who might have known Harold. So, on a trip to Oakland, California to visit my biological father, I met a very tall, dark, and handsome man named Joseph Dubuclet, affectionately known as "Duby." He was a seaman, and when he was on shore, he hung around with the SF/Oakland Bay area Black elites. He was a much sought-after eligible bachelor of thirty-eight years when we met.

He was originally from Louisiana but had left home when he was seventeen after a quarrel with his father, and joined the Navy. We dated for a while; him coming to Los Angeles and me going to visit him in San Francisco. I was soon sick of this arrangement, so one day I told him "either s—- or get off the pot." He laughed so hard, and he said he told everybody what I had said. But in short order he asked me to marry him; I said yes, and we were married in 1959. This was his first marriage and, of course, my second.

Duby Relocating to Los Angeles

Because Duby was often out to sea for long periods of time, and my support system for my children and good job were all in Los Angeles, we decided that it was best to live in Los Angeles.

This move proved disastrous for Duby. He was not able to get a ship out of LA because of the tight and clannish Southern CA Longshoremen union. In addition, he didn't seem to fit in with the LA crowd. He, like most California Bay Area Northerners, thought that the Bay area was more cosmopolitan and sophisticated, especially San Francisco, and that Los Angeles, in spite of Hollywood, was just a big spread out "cow town."

Although he took a job in the Aerospace industry (North America Aviation) and he worked for a short time for the LA County Juvenile System and even had his own "Handy Man Business," he was a seaman at heart, and he was very unhappy, and he missed the sea, which had been his life since he was seventeen. We both agreed that he should go back up to the Bay area and try to catch a ship out. He did go back for a short time, but he said that he missed me and the kids so much that he came back to Los Angeles and took a job again in the Aerospace industry.

In spite of his unhappiness, Duby tried his best to be a good father to Carol and Ronnie and took an interest in their upbringing. The thing that did make him very happy was the birth of his first and only child, a son, DiJon Dubuclet, born November 1961. We both really wanted this child, and now I was complete. I had the three children I always said I wanted.

We lived in my parent's duplex or back house while we waited to buy our own home. Duby thought we should wait for a while until we bought our own home. However, I was tired of living in that duplex, even though it was nice. Duby was too laidback for me, and I was too progressive and probably too assertive for him.

But I had waited long enough; I needed a house for my children.

Ronnie was staying in the front house with Mama and Carol with me. One day in 1959, a friend of mine told me about a nice house in a nice neighborhood on East Ninetieth Street in Los Angeles. I told Duby that I thought that we should buy this house. He did not say yes, but he did not say no either, so I called my biological father to see if he would help us with the down payment. I told him we needed $1500 for the down payment. He said that he would think about it.

In a few days I heard back, and he told me that he had gone to the bank, and the banker had told him it was not a good idea to loan money to family. I didn't get upset. I just said, "Thank you, Daddy, for trying." Well, this was a setback, but it was not going to stop me from getting this house.

What I learned

I believe that I learned several valuable lessons during this period in my life: First that a man has to be on his own turf, so to speak, the place where he believes he has surer footing and control. Especially if he has to provide for a family.

Even in this day and time most men will not choose to be on a women's turf if he can at all help it. Men have just been enculturated that way, and I do not believe this will ever change.

I have learned that from a man's perspective "turf and being sure-footed" is tied in with his "self-respect," and respect to a man may be more important than anything else in a relationship. Duby was on my turf in Los Angeles, and it made him unhappy, and it was not good for the marriage.

Second, I learned that you do not ever have to take "NO" as an answer if you really want something, because "where there is a will there is a way." I wanted a house and to do better for my family, and I was not taking "no" from anyone as an answer, and my perseverance paid off.

Chapter 12

Nothing Down

Though the idea of "Nothing Down" became popular in the nineties, I was naively practicing it back in the fifties. When I did not get the loan from Daddy I needed, I went to talk to Mr. Hartcroft, the owner of the house I was trying to purchase and he agreed to carry the papers. The bank came out and completed an appraisal, which was below what the owner had wanted, but he accepted the appraisal anyway. I told Duby that we could get the house because Mr. Harcroft, the owner, was going to carry the papers. He was skeptical, but I assured him that this was the case, so off we went to escrow.

When the escrow Lady asked us what we were putting down, I said with certainty that Mr. Harcroft is carrying the note. The escrow clerk looked annoyed and said forcefully, I know that, but what are you putting down? I replied just as forcefully. I asked, Mr. Harcroft did you not say you were carrying the paper? Mr. Harcroft answered in a very strong and slow drawn out voice and heavy accent, "Yes, that's what I said."

By this time Duby was looking up and around at the ceiling as if he was thinking "what has this crazy wife of mine done now?" By now, the escrow woman was so frustrated because she now understood that I did not have a down payment. She just closed her folder and said in a very irritated manner, I will need to talk to my boss about this. It was now late Friday evening. So, I had to listen to Naysayer Duby and agonize over what the bank would do the whole weekend. I never stopped praying and believing that I would have favor. As soon as I thought the bank (Broadway Federal Savings) was opened on Monday morning, I called and lo and behold the bank had approved the transaction, and I was told to come for the closing. (God's favor). I needed $600.00 for the closing. I was always saving money for the children, so I decided I could use some of their money.

I used $600.00 for closing and $28.00 went toward a truck to move us. Since I had been successful in pulling off the "Nothing Down" coup, despite Duby's negative attitude, he became obstinate and said he was not going to move. Well, the truck was there and things were being loaded up with the help of Papa Leamon, Mama, and the kids. When Duby saw that we were moving anyway, he decided he better come along after all. We all had a big laugh about his ninety-degree turn. Once we were settled in the house, Duby made it into a beautiful home. He had construction and remodeling talents I knew nothing about.

What I learned

I learned that you can have what you ask for if you believe in your heart and don't doubt you can have what you say. The Holy scripture in Mark 23-24 quote Jesus as saying, "Truly I tell you that if anyone says to this mountain, 'Be lifted up and thrown into the sea,' and has no doubt in his heart but believes that it will happen, it will be done for him.

Therefore I tell you, whatever you ask in prayer, believe that you have received it, and it will be yours.... I prayed for God's favor in the situation and believed somehow I would have it even though I did not know how; and God's favor I received.I learned that it is important not to allow others to steal your faith and joy. It does not matter if others around you cannot see the miracle as long as you believe.

Faith is believing in what you cannot see. The Holy scripture says that Now faith is confidence in what we hope for and assurance about what we do not see. Hebrews 11:1

Chapter 13

Entrepreneurship

I always had a spirit of entrepreneurship. I can remember always loving to sell and make money. This was in large part due to helping Mama and Papa Leamon in their café business back in Fort Worth when I was a preteen.

In junior high one summer when I saw an LA work crew laying water pipes in my neighbor, I decided to make sandwiches and drinks and sell it to them at lunch. This was a hit.

More than making money I loved managing money. Mama and Papa Leamon allowed me to handle the family budget while in high school. After I paid the bills and bought groceries, I could use what was left for me. Believe me, I always made sure something was left over for the new trendy clothes I loved so much. Mama and Papa Leamon would laugh about how I was feeding them the same thing over and over and cutting corners on the food.

As I recounted earlier, I also did the banking for the Jewish Milliner back in 1939 and worked as a cashier for Lerners, bookkeeper for Nate Diamond, and others.

I always loved to be on the business management and accounting end of things, even though I had no formal training in the area. But what I desired most was to have a Women's clothing business. I began taking Home Study courses via mail in fashion design from the National Academy of Dress Design in Chicago. Owning that dress shop was always in the back of mind. I even went to LA Metropolitan and took a class in tailoring and pattern making so that I would have a better understanding of dress making.

Starting a Home Clothing Business

A clothing business was always a dream of mine. I always had an interest in women's fashion and had a flare, I thought, for dressing fashionably and enjoyed seeing others who dressed fashionably. I had also worked in several women's apparel shops along Central Avenue in its heyday and at the downtown millinery manufacturer that I talked about earlier. I became very interested in the retail end of business for myself. With the encouragement from Mr. Albert Peake, who owned the largest women's retail store in the Black community during that time, I was able to pursue this interest. Mr. Peake was also the first Black to sell women's apparel from door-to-door like the Jewish salesmen during that time. He often sold to Mama.

One day when he came to sell Mama clothing, I told him that I was interested in selling. He said that I could start by selling hosiery for myself, so he took me to downtown Los Angeles and introduced me to the Owner/Manager of Beverly Hills Hosiery. The company was established in Los Angeles in 1934 and is still in business to this day with several other new locations. The owners seemed to like me right away (God's Favor Again).

They sold the merchandise to me at wholesale, and I resold it at retail using Mr. Peake's retail license. Mr. Peake even allowed me to set up his first business office near Western Avenue in Los

Angeles. I started out selling hose, but later sold lingerie all by appointment. Although I transported the merchandised in my car, I always sold by appointment. I would often take Ronnie and Carol with me. I would bring their lunch and toys so that they could entertain themselves while I was making sales.

Later I started having fashion shows on my lunch hour at work. My supervisor did not seem to mind. Women would come on their lunchtime to see the clothing I would put out. The clothing was from Mr. Peake. Later this grew into home fashion shows where I would, along with my daughter, Carol, and my new daughter-in-law, Janice (Ronnie's wife) put on weekly shows in various homes.

The arrangement that I had with Mr. Peak was that I would retain twenty percent of all sales. I would get maybe four dresses at a time and sell them, then four more and on and on until I decided to go directly to the wholesalers myself.

After then big trucks would pull up in front of my house on East Ninetieth Street to drop off merchandise. The home business grew, and I even paid my young son, Dijon, $5.00 per month to use his bedroom to house the racks of clothing. We used the living room as the showroom.

I eventually hired three other saleswomen and offered them the same arrangement I had with Mr. Peak, which was twenty percent of the sales price.

I wanted to set up charge accounts for women who needed to "buy on time," so a young man like my son, Donald Matthews, who grew up with my son Ronnie was interested in helping me in the business, so he loaned me $1500 without interest to put aside for this purpose. The business prospered and grew right there in the family living room.

I learned a lot from Mr. Peak about the retail clothing business and credit him entirely for getting me started. Always trying to better myself, when I heard that there were volunteers from SCORE (Small Business Administration Services Core of Retired Executives) I sought their assistance to acquire further business knowledge and skills.

The Birth of CJ Elegance

It was always my plan to have my daughter Carolyn Jo to be a successful business woman. I believe that women can be successful at any level in the corporate world. I could see that she had great potential and skills to be successful in the retail clothing business so on her twenty-first birthday, I told her why don't we become business partners. As a matter of fact, I asked her "Can I be your business partner?" This was also a way to appease her when her friends were getting cars and she was not.

We had also talk about names for the business, and at first I thought about something with my name "Orlean" since people always associated it with New Orlean but decided against it. Carol and I sat and looked through magazines looking for the right name. I then said to Carol, what about your name? So Carol named it after herself Carol Jo hence the name became "CJ Elegance." I could see that I was now on the road to having the women's dress boutique I had always dreamed of, even as a teenager.

After we settled on a name, I took Carol down to get the business license and set up the business organization. I never like seeing people having their children in business working under them so I made sure that we really were partners. The ownership would be 60/40 with me retaining the controlling interest.

Obviously, I would have to make the full investment and acquire the lines of credit since Carol was still a young girl of twenty-one without credit history or resources.

Carol worked hard alongside me to make the business work and so did my daughter-in-law Janice, Ronnie's wife. Although we were still running the business from the house, the dream was always to have a dress shop in a good location. That was to come but first, I needed a way to bankroll this dream.

Chapter 14

Finding a Way to Bankroll My Dream

Somewhere during my stint with the Unity Project, which I will discuss later, I met a business women affiliated with the Unity Project who interested me in a property investment. She had found this property with eight family houses and needed $4,000 to acquire the property.

I came up with the $4,000 for the down payment, and we agreed to be business partners and that she would be the partner responsible for managing the property. Well, as time went on, she stopped using the rental income to pay the loan. She even told the bank that she had been robbed of the funds. However, after the bank investigated and found out that this was not true, they had a meeting with us.

Since I had been the one who had made the down payment, and she had not invested anything, the bank managers decided to have her name removed from the loan and put the loan in my name only giving me the eight properties. Not only that, the bank Cabrillo Savings and Loan mangers seem to take a liking to me so whenever there was a foreclosure, they would contact me (God's Favor Again).

On one such occasion, I told them I wanted the property that they were offering me but did not have the down payment however if they would hear me out, I had a plan on how I could make that happen. So in a meeting with them I explained, using my pad and pencil (which I always seem to have) that if they would allow me to withhold payment on the mortgages I had with them for two months, I could take that money and put toward the down and would catch the other mortgages up before foreclosure. They both started laughing so hard and looked at me as if I was from Mars. They couldn't believe that I was telling them to their face that I was intentionally not going to pay my mortgages so I could buy this property they were offering me. But after they finish laughing at me, they said that they would consider my harebrained scheme and so they did and I got the property and later other pieces. (God's Favor Again)

The managers said they would like to see me with 100 pieces of property, but because I did not have the family support for that kind of venture, unfortunately, I never got that far. However, what I did have were the resources to invest in my dream to own a women's dress shop.

What I learned

I learned that you must believe in yourself and see your own ideas. Like at Ralph Waldo Emmerson said in his essay Self Reliance. He said, "To believe your own thoughts, to believe that what is true for you in your private heart is true for all men—that is genius."

In other words, don't dismiss your own thoughts or harebrained schemes someone else like the two bank managers might just think that they are brilliant or at least makes a lot of sense. My greatest lesson was again "Where there is a will there is a way."

Chapter 15

Giving My All to My Community

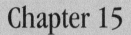

While still working for the City of Los Angeles and at the same time running the home clothing business, I was approached by the founder of the Unity Project Olton Bluion to join him and others to launch a project to help revitalize the business community in South Central Los Angeles. So I took a leave of absence from the City and joined others to help launch the Unity project. The Unity Project - Unity Services Corporation

Just before the 1965 "Watts's riot" or Civil Unrest there was a concern from within the community to address the current economic disparity and lack of community-owned businesses. Businesses once owned by Blacks, and there were many, seemed to have died with their owner. The Civil Unrest just intensified the need to address these issues more quickly.

One of the projects designed to create new black ownership was the Unity Project spearheaded by a community activist and visionary, Olton Bluion. And after years of planning by community leaders in South Central Los Angeles and Compton the Unity Service Corporation was established. Unity was established to provide consumer services, economic and employment opportunities to the community.

Unity Services Corporation had several entities: two supermarkets, credit union, and two automotive gasoline service centers. A restaurant, dry cleaner, and a childcare center were to follow.

Community participation was encouraged through the sale of shares at $10.00 per share with a $200 maximum investment per person. The community was elated over this new opportunity, and people came from all over LA to lend support. People also came from other countries to see how they could replicate this project in their urban neighborhood. Atty. General Robert Kennedy came to visit the project for the same reason.

Many persons like myself left long-established jobs to come and help out the community.

I was hired as the Director of the Credit Union and put my whole heart and soul into this job to the point of near exhaustion.

I spent countless hours away from home to ensure that the Credit Union ran efficiently, many times compromising the time I spent with my family.

I wouldn't leave until I could account for every penny. I recall one night as I was trying to balance the receipts and the Vice President had to stay until I was done. He was so tired of waiting, so he asked very timidly what was the amount that I needed to balance. I said ten cents. That seemed to have infuriated him, and he asked, "Are you telling me that we have been here all this time so that you can find a dime?" He said, "Hell, if that is all you need, here it is," and he went into his pocket and pulled out a dime. We both started laughing so hard and couldn't seem to stop. I must admit that I was overly committed to making everything right not only at the Credit Union but the whole project. I kept thinking that if we can make this project work, all of our children could benefit and the sacrifice I was making would be well worth it.

Needing Outside Help and Expertise

In addition to my position as the Director of the Credit Union, I also served as a member of the Community Board. During some challenging times, Olton Blouin, Chairman of the Board and I would almost come to blows during the meetings because he would not listen to members' request for outside expertise.

"Blouin," as we called him, was an extraordinarily brilliant man, but he was extremely stubborn and would not hear of getting outside help, although me and my only comrade in this endeavor—our young accountant, Calvin Harrison—begged him to do so. In Blouin's mind it would appear that as Blacks we were not up to the task. Although Blouin was truly a visionary and an excellent spokesman for the organization, operational management was not his strong suit and we needed management consultation especially with running the markets.

Even though we had wooed a manager of one of the most popular supermarket chains to manage the Unity supermarkets, things went terribly wrong. The manager lacked the operational experience that was needed. In addition, the markets were being sabotaged by the Certified Grocers who would see to it that our produce was being delayed, plus allegedly there had been a meeting about how they could make us fail.

Unfortunately, these tactics were successful, so along with the decline in support from the community, the markets got into real trouble. In addition to the sabotage, the market had a high incidence of theft. When I heard that some of the employees were walking out with groceries that they did not pay for, especially at night, I told my husband, Duby, that I was going down there and put a stop to it.

He tried to dissuade me, but his plea fell on deaf ears. "The Josephine" had come out, so in the car we went. When we got to the market, I stood in front of the exit doorway and asked kindly to see the receipts of everyone coming from the market with a package. When they couldn't produce a receipt, I told them to "march right back in the store and put the items on the counter." No one resisted my demand. Even though I weighed only about 120 pounds. I was so angry that I felt like I weighed two tons and was ready to take on anyone. My poor husband, Duby, couldn't believe my boldness and stood close just in case someone tried to take on his crazy wife and he would have to intervene. Eventually the markets closed.

There were several contributing factors to the failure of the markets, namely, the Certified Grocers who blatantly sabotaged the store by not delivering the groceries on time followed by the lack of community support, and inadequate management, and most of all the failure to obtain the outside expertise needed.

After the markets closed, so did the service stations and finally the Credit Union. Members would invest small amounts and then borrow twice that much and not pay it back. In addition, they would get bad car loans. Eventually the whole enterprise ended up in bankruptcy.

I was very upset with Bluion for not getting the help I kept telling him we needed. As the Holy scripture says "Pride comes before a fall." I took the failure personally; not only as a Board member, and Director of the Credit Union but as a member of the community.

I just naively thought that I could "save my community" and make it financially successful. In the end I was the only member of the Board of Directors willing to come before the media to talk about the failure of the Unity Project. The failure of the enterprise took such a toll on me that I had to be hospitalized for two weeks for exhaustion, and it took additional weeks in the house with the blinds closed to recuperate.

What I learned

There are many important things I learned from this experience, some business related and others very personal.

First no man is an island, especially in a business or corporate venture therefore reach quickly for consultation from experts or from other successful business entities long before you get into trouble. Have resources readily available; identify them in your business plan so you know who to call upon them when you need help.

The Holy scripture says that pride comes before the fall. Pride kept the project from reaching outside of the community. Race, color, nationality, or personal or social preferences do not matter when you need help. Also be willing to pay for it when necessary. I know that there are more sophisticated business approaches and models, however I am just sharing what I learned.

What I learned

Second, call out your saboteurs. We allowed forces like the Grocery Union to quietly sabotage the project and failed to inform the community of what was happening or to get their help. Healthy competition is one thing, but sabotage is quite another. Exposing the saboteurs would have helped.

Third, playing up the individual ownership. Little was done to make a big deal that the project was owned by the community who actually owned shares in the project. There is a reason why big chains like Costco and others have a big sign saying the business is employee-owned. It ensures that if I own part of it, I should support it.

On a personal note, I learned that no matter how much you are dedicated to a purpose or project it must be balanced with family life. Few if any sacrifices that people made for work professional or nonprofessional where family relationships are compromised have good results. Next, I paid a personal physical price for thinking that I alone could make the project successful when I did not know when to let go. No one wants to lose or be a part of failure when they have known success, however, I have learned that you must be willing to cut your losses and move on.

Chapter 16

Life After Unity: CJ Elegance

While I was recuperating from the disappointment related to the failure of the Unity Project, which took three to four months and after I decided not to return to my position at the City of LA, I decided that I would return to selling clothes full time . So, for the next two years we sold clothes from the house. Somewhere along the way I developed Meniere's disease an inner ear disorder that causes episodes of extreme dizziness. I was actually crawling around on the floor and had to direct Carol what to do as well as have her console DiJon who was very angry because I was not myself. I knew it was time to move out of the house into a shop and that it was time to expand the clothing business that we were currently operating from the house and acquire my dream of a women's clothing store.

Because I was still reeling from the inner-ear condition, I asked my husband, Duby, and Carol, my partner in the business, to go and find a space where we could relocate the shop. The retail location they found was on West Slauson on the west side of Los Angeles. Duby did most all of the work to remodel the shop the way we wanted. The shop still remains in the same location fifty years later but with a new facelift.

Although it was 1970, area businesses were predominately white-owned. The owner of the conclave of shops where we had chosen our new location did not want to rent to us because we were Black but finally did at $150 per month, a rate greater than what white shop owners in the conclave were paying at the time.

The affluent predominantly Black neighborhoods of View Park, Windsor Hills, Baldwin Hills, and Ladera were within walking distance to the shop so we had a great clientele. Not just from these neighborhoods but from all over South Los Angeles and South Central Los Angeles. Affluent and non-affluent alike patronized the shop along with many Black celebrities and politicians. We not only sold one-of-a-kind fashion but held fashions shows and had other activities related to fashion and later home design, which Carol had a real flare for.

I personally saw the shop and dressing my Black sisters as a kind of ministry, so it was a lot of "praise the Lord" going on in the shop.

The atmosphere was of love, caring, and fun. I made sure that all of the finances stayed in order, and I made sure that my daughter and daughter-in-law were paid even when I wasn't. Even though there was a 60/40 interest, I split everything down the middle with my daughter and except for what was on paper in reality we were equal partners.

Carol focused mainly on the clothing, design and buyer's aspect of the business, and I, as usual, handled the finances and all of the bookkeeping. I can now brag and say that in the forty-plus years that I was intimately involved with the business, I did not bounce one check or ever not make employee payroll. I kept every vendor happy, even in slow times. I always wanted to stay abreast and acquire new business management skills, which I did by taking business management classes from the UCLA and USC Extension programs, and as I mentioned earlier availing myself to the knowledge and skills provided by volunteers from SCORE (Small Business Administration Services Core of Retired Executives.

After some years Carol wanted to expand to another location farther west. Well, I was not necessarily enthusiastic about it, because I knew from my own life experiences in race relations that Blacks patronized Blacks. Few patrons in most known Black business are from other races. The same is probably true among other nonwhite businesses as well. However, this was the eighties, and I did not want my daughter to ever see limitations in what she wanted to do, and so, I agreed. Well, unfortunately I was right, and we lost significant capital and ended up closing the business in the other location. We then put all of that energy into the main location, and Carol and I spent many hours planning new activities for the business.

CJ Elegance was not to be just another women's dress shop. I wanted it to have some type of community outreach. So we used it as a launching pad for fashion shows with well-known fashion models. We were involved with other things as well. In the early years, along with Regency East Design, we represented the Black community specialty stores in the "Fashion Across America," which featured designers throughout the country. The boutique also outfitted participants in the LA Sentinel/Golden State Mutual Mother of the Year benefit.

The boutique attracted and began dressing black stars from popular sitcoms such as "2-2-7" and "That's My Mama." When the acclaimed Oscar Winner, Regina King was getting ready for her prom and graduation. CJ Elegance was her choice for dress.

Many celebrities visited our boutique including A visit in 1981 from the editor of *Essence Magazine*, Susan Taylor.

(Left to Right) Orlean, Susan Taylor, Carol and Janice
(LA Sentinel Newspaper)

The boutique was as involved with community activities as it was with the business of selling. I enjoyed living my dream with my daughter. I was also able to share my zest for living and my belief that "Where there is a will there is a way" with clients and other business associates when they would ask for advice or felt like they needed to share personal concerns. It became almost like a ministry of "it is possible to live your dream no matter how small or large because "where there is a will there is a way."

ORLEAN DUBUCLET—A gift of four dresses on Carol Jo's birthday has yielded a very lucrative family business. The boutique is called C.J.'s Elegance.—PHOTO NARESHIMAH OSEI

LA Sentinel Newspaper Orlean living her dream
(LA Sentinel Newspaper)

ORLEAN DUBUCLET, CAROL SHAW
Owners C.J. Elegance

SHEER ELEGANCE—Energetic mother, daughter team, Orlean Dubuclet, bottom, and daughter Carol Jo,

Orlean and Carol Received Industry Award 2019
The Juanita A. Portlock Memorial Scholarship Fund

■ In **40** years, Orlean Dubuclet and Carolyn Jo Shaw grew C.J.'s Elegance into a small local dress boutique with a big reputation. /OW photo by Cynthia E. Griffin.

Article LA Sentinel Newspaper

CJ Elegance Celebrates 50 Years
1967-2019

A Time to Leave

When my daughter and partner wanted to take the business in a new direction, I did not stand in the way, even though I could have. I am not saying it was easy to step aside because it was probably one of the hardest things I have ever done. But my daughter had worked hard in the business and deserved to see what she could do on her own. I am never one to stand in the way of progress.

I still, however, insisted on being involved in the financial and accounting end of the business. However, in 2012 at the ripe old age of eighty-seven, still in excellent physical and mental health, I reluctantly gave up the manual bookkeeping to a contracted accountant so that the accounting data could be computerized.

Under my daughter's leadership and management the business has expanded to include other entrepreneurship activities. Among the many social media presentations showcasing the business is an online shopping gallery featuring clothing and accessories by up and coming designers. The business seems to be moving right along under my daughter's management, and I am very proud of her accomplishments. As mentioned earlier , this year the business celebrates its fiftieth-year anniversary and will become one of the oldest if not the oldest black family owned women's retail clothing business in the Los Angeles area.

I have always had hope that after Carol retires that the business would stay in the family and perhaps one of the granddaughters would be interested in perpetuating my dream.

Leaving and Staying Relevant

Timing in life means everything and at the age of eighty-seven, it was time for me to move on to the next phase of my life's work.

I still kept my fingers in the financial and accounting end of the business, which I was always good at. I enjoyed creative financing (in a good way) and keeping the business on a solid foundation.

I have always tried to stay current so when I was eighty-five years old, I took a computer class, and I still stay abreast of all the business happenings through business publications and other related media business programs.

Self-Ordained Financial Consultant

Probably to the annoyance of some and the intrigue of others, I have become a self-ordained voluntary informal consultant to anyone trying to get their finances in order or life back on track. I do this by phone, in person, and on my daily morning walks. I enjoy sharing my wisdom and life experiences, and the you know "where there is a will there is a way" slogan. When I was no longer involved with the business, for a short while, I involved myself with a young woman who was trying to start a clothing business.

Involving Myself with My Grandchildren and Great-Grandchildren

I also became involved with my grandchildren's school activities going on field trips and helping out where I was allowed. When I could no longer be relevant with my grandchildren, I got involved in my great-grandchildren's school, doing fundraising and accompanying the students on field trips.

The school staff always seemed happy to see me and have me participate, and I enjoyed being a Great-grandmother superstar. I was even written up in the school's yearbook.

What I learned

Knowing when to leave and remaining relevant are akin to each other. Timing is everything in all relationships whether personal, political, business, or professional. Knowing when to leave is paramount. You always want to leave when you are on top when at all possible. There is nothing like feeling a sense of accomplishment. Have you ever seen people like sports figures, politicians, and entertainers who don't know when to leave?

I can't say that leaving something that I loved so much was easy especially, when you can still contribute. However, don't be hesitant to pass the torch and go and light a fire someplace else.

I had learned many simple but successful business strategies that I could pass on to others starting in the business. Such as:

1. How to soft market to potential clientele through involvement in community activities and hosting various social events, like the fashion shows we sponsored.

2. How to maintain a solid clientele base by always having quality and timely fashionable merchandise and knowing what is in your client's wardrobe and not selling them things that they do not need, just to make a sale.

What I learned

3. The importance of maintaining a warm, customer friendly atmosphere and attractive surroundings and making the clientele feel beautiful and good about themselves.

4. Knowing how to keep the vendors happy by paying on time even when it is not the full invoice.

5. Seeking outside help if you need it. Whether it is a class or merely speaking with other colleagues in the business.

Some successful companies allow retirees with special expertise to serve as consultants until the replacements find out where the bathrooms are located, so to speak. However, if that's not the case, there are other ways to use your talent you don't just go home and die. As long as you have breath, make some contribution if nothing more than sharing a word of wisdom on the phone or internet or on your daily walk.

Chapter 17

My Family

Mama

As the only child of my mother, my relationship with her has been the most significant relationship of my life. As you can see throughout my story, she influenced my life in extraordinary ways to say the least. I was blessed and favored to have had her with me most of my life. She was also an extraordinary grandmother and great-grandmother as well.

Mama age 38

Mama died in 1991 at the ripe old age of eighty-six, still standing up fighting for someone. She was not above allowing what I call "The Josephine" to come out when she felt she needed to get someone "straight" so to speak.

When I have used the phrase "The Josephine came out in me" it was in reference to how Mama would have handled things had she been in the same situation because Mama did not allow anyone to run over her.

Her obituary described her as a self-ordained advocate volunteering and advocating for numerous civic and political causes. On the very day she became ill and was hospitalized for the final time, she was trying to help someone whose property was being taken away from her. She never stopped trying to help people.

She was forever calling city hall and complaining about something that the community or someone needed. The

councilman for our district, which was the Ninth District, was Gilbert Lindsey, who was elected as the first Black councilman in Los Angeles and served from 1963–1999. Momma kept him and his staff busy about what was needed for South Los Angeles.

Mama in her later years

Mama never allowed her limited education to stop her from making a decent living or advocating for others. When she left her various housekeeping jobs, which she had for many years, she became the first Black Avon Sales lady in the area. When she could no longer go from door to door, she sold Avon from her house.

It was important for her to stay in her home when she became sick and disabled, and it was my pleasure to help Papa Leamon take care of her in her old age. She was a mighty force to deal with, and I hope that this apple did not fall far from the tree.

Papa Leamon

Although I maintained a relationship with my biological father, in reality Papa Leamon was the constant father figure in my life. Papa Leamon lived for six years after Mama died. He was a stalwart of a man. He along with Mama were my bedrock.

Papa Leamon

Papa Leamon always treated me as his daughter not as his stepdaughter. He was extremely industrious and, like Mama, he was a "first" or among the first to do something as a Black person. Papa Leamon was the first Black to be hired in the labor force at North America Aviation in 1941.

As a matter of fact, we would get a big laugh because when they showed the Employee Orientation promo, Papa Leamon was the only "token Black." He took advantage of his time at North America Aviation. He went there as part of the Maintenance Crew, but very early he went to Trade School and received a certificate in Air Conditioning, Refrigeration, and Ventilation. He was highly respected by the company, mainly because of the many winning suggestions that he would put into the company's "suggestion box." Some were very significant and impactful, saving the company money and other resources.

Papa Leamon receiving an award at North America Aviation (Rockwell Intl (Boeing)

In addition to receiving awards like the one he is receiving in the picture above, he also received bonus checks much to the delight of Mama and me. He was also instrumental at one point in getting jobs with the company for both of my husbands as well as other Black men in the community.

When Papa Leamon required respite care away from home . I found the very best place I could for him. He died knowing that I was always there for him. I went to see him every day no matter how tired I was. Often when I went to visit him, I would sit in his wheelchair and fall asleep. He didn't mind. He was comforted by the fact that I was there with him. He and Mama were always there for me, and I was always there for them.

My Biological Daddy

I have spoken earlier about my father and my relationship with him during my early childhood. However, as I reflect upon my life, it is amazing how much I loved my father, even though he did not raise me. Mama was careful never to say anything bad about my father to me; that way I could maintain good memories about him. I fondly remember how, as a little girl visiting him after he and Mama divorced, I would just love sitting in his lap looking up and just saying, "Daddy." For some reason that was so special to me.

When we moved away to California, I made it my business to know where my father was. I kept up with him even when he did not keep up with me. No matter, I always felt that he loved me.

Eventually when I was an adult he moved to Northern California, and I could visit him. As a matter of fact, it was on such a visit that I met my husband, Duby.

I could never be angry or disappointed with my father even when he did not loan me the money for a down payment for a house, even though he could have. Because he said the banker told him when he went to get the money to never loan to relatives.

I do recall that on occasion when speaking with him on the phone, I said, "Daddy I do not have one thing in my home that came from you." He said nothing, however, in about a week, I received many boxes from him and inside was the most beautiful fine china, crystal, and silverware I had ever seen, which I have to this day.

Daddy (Steve Wilson)

What I learned

I learned that God loved me so much that he gave me Mama to ensure that my life's purpose would not be thwarted along the way. Her role, while meeting her own life's purpose of helping others, was to mirror to me my life's purpose, which was to do the same and care about and help others.

I learned that parents are put in our lives to serve as a compass to warn us about the future, and that we should always listen because no matter how ragged their lives may or may not be, God has endowed them with the wisdom to keep us from harm. Mama taught me to acknowledge God, to trust him, and that he would never leave me alone. She also taught me to be tough and to stand up for myself and others.

I learned that God gave me Papa Leamon to serve as the bedrock for Mama and to be a "soft landing" for me when I needed one.

I learned that children have a peculiar attachment to biological parents even when they are not in their lives. It was always important for me to keep up with my biological father, even when he did not keep up with me.

I loved him unconditionally.

Half Siblings (Daddy's Children)

Beatrice

I always maintained a relationship with my half sister, Beatrice, and always regretted that she was never able to come to live with Mama and me or come to California when I went to get her.

My brother, Iteamer, I only saw once in life. After the one time, we only kept in touch through letter writing. Unfortunately, we eventually lost contact. I did always make an effort to keep up with what was happening with him through others.

My Husband

My second husband, Joseph Rudolph Ducublet (Duby), and I were married for thirty-nine years. I spoke earlier about how we met and about his challenges in transitioning from his life at sea and from the San Francisco Bay Area to Los Angeles and how hard he tried to be a good stepfather to Carol and Ronnie and how proud he was of his son DiJon.

However, he really never became his old self again until we moved from the old neighborhood. I loved the old neighborhood, especially the immediate community around East Ninetieth Street, but we needed to be closer to the shop and to Dijon's school.

Once we got the house in the new neighborhood, Duby became stubborn and said he wasn't going to move because basically he did not fully support the idea of moving. However, contrary to what he felt about moving, he was slowly refurbishing the new house for the move, but it seemed that he was deliberately dragging it out. He was taking so long that my son Dijon thought it was foolish, so one Saturday he got a friend and just started moving us. I woke up and said, "What are you doing?" and he said, "Moving us," and I joined in. Duby didn't come right away, even though the old house had been sold.

But after a month, he moved over and basically changed into a different person. He was now in what he called his "San Francisco Bay element" and became very popular with the new neighbors.

I would come home from the shop and he would be holding "court" in the garage with the new neighbors. I had never seen him so happy. He was the star of the neighborhood. Now that Duby had found his place again we had many pleasurable and wonderful times together. He also became a doting grandfather and actually became the babysitter for his youngest grandchildren Khari and Maleena. We enjoyed life together until his death in 1997 at the age of seventy-five.

Duby and Orlean

My Children

Children are a blessing from God, even though we may not always feel that way, especially when we do not agree with what they choose to do and be in life. Kahil Gilbran in his work titled "The Profit" addresses this very concern. When asked about children the following is a few lines of what he had to say about children:

> "They are the sons and daughters of
> Life's longing for itself.
> They come through you but not from you
> And though they are with you yet they
> Belong not to you.
> You may give them your love but not your thoughts.
> For they have their own thoughts..." (Gibran, 1973)

Roland Merchant Sr. in his book on parenting and training Titled" Passion Sustained Commitment To Excellence " Asserts that:

> "The family inevitably is the model for the child's
> values , beliefs, attitudes and moral codes and

provides the initial interpretation of the meaning of life. Children usually measure who they are by the family standards" (Merchant 2012).

God blessed me with three children. Harold Washington III (Ronnie) and Carolyn Jo (Carol) from my first marriage to Harold Washington Jr. and Dijon (DD) from my second marriage to Joseph Dubuclet. I tell my children often that none of them were mistakes. They were all very much wanted,

All of my children have some of my character traits or reflect my personality in some way.

My oldest son, Harold, has my compassion and love for people. He loves helping people. This is a trait he has shown all of his life. Since he was just a little boy, he was always very protective of me and that has never changed. Like me, Ronnie is a fighter and persistent and very persuasive when he strongly believes in something.

My daughter, Carolyn Jo, has my love for fashion and entrepreneurship and will not take "no" as an answer. Always a leader and growing up she was my confidante and was like a little mother to Dijon when he was growing up.

My youngest son, Dijon, has my "no nonsense" approach to just about everything especially business and real estate and is a good steward of resources. When he was in college, I would give him motivational tapes to play when he was commuting to and from school. I do believe that it paid off.

I am blessed to this very day to have all three of my children "there for me". Each one in their own way see after me even when I don't need them to. Which is a great testimony I hope to my sacrifice and investment in their lives.

Child Rearing

Because Mama on her meager income did not let me want for anything that was important to me, I vowed to do the same for my children even if it meant sacrificing, which often it did. For a brief time, I was a single parent but worked extra hard to see that my children did not miss out on anything that would make their childhood happy. I tried to expose them to various things that I felt would broaden their horizons, including piano lessons, even if it was a struggle because I knew "where there is a will there is a way."

Family Budget

I always had the kids when they were growing up to work with me on the family budget. Once a month I would sit with the oldest two Ronnie and Carol at the time and would show them the amount of money I had coming in.

Together we would pay the bills and what was left over after necessities, we could have for entertainment or to buy something they wanted. Involving them in the budget allowed them to have a greater appreciation about money management and budgetary constraints. To this very day, I live by a budget. As I mentioned earlier, I started appreciating living by a budget as a teenager when Mama and Papa Leamon allowed me to handle the family's budget.

What I learned

I have learned that allowing children to have "hands on" with the family budget is an excellent way for them to learn money management and budgetary constraints. That way they know not to ask for things if it is not in the family budget. They know what is coming in and what has to be paid out. They can handle it way better than you think. Whether you have little or much, the principles are the same.

Don't say "well our budget is too large or complicated;" nothing these days is complicated for our children to grasp. Remember this is the age of a knowledge explosion with all kinds of accounting programs online that they probably understand better than you.

Rather than having your kids saying "my parents can't afford this or that, they can simply say it's not in our family budget this month."

The family budget is the responsibility of the entire family, not just the parents. It also a good way for children to understand the value of money.

Educating the Children

If parents have to make any sacrifices, it must be in trying to provide the best education possible for their children. Today with the advent of technology and the knowledge explosion on the internet, parents have many supplemental and supportive educational options for their children that I did not have when I was raising my children.

Parents used to be able to say "I don't have time to take my children to the library or to get the supplemental help that my child needs." Now the internet is a learning lab. You can almost do self-learning in every subject online.

I wanted my children to have the best education that was available to me at the time. As a single parent for a period of time, I felt that I needed help with providing them with a structured environment that mirrored what I was trying to teach them at home, so even when times were tough, with the help of Mama, I managed to keep Ronnie and Carol in private parochial (Catholic) school because I thought it would the best environment for them during this time.

I realize that there were good public schools, but I was just trying to do my best and provide them with what I thought was the *environment* that would support them the most. However, by the time DiJon, my youngest son, was in the fifth grade, our business was in an area where there were great public schools so he attended public schools there afterwards.

Like many parents I sacrificed to made sure that the children were able to participate in any school activity that they desired. So the kids were involved in all kinds of sports and other extracurricular activities. I made sure that they were exposed to life outside of school by taking them to all kinds of events and places that fitted into that family budget that they help make. We did not live in an affluent neighborhood when they were growing up, so it meant keeping them busy and away from negative influences as much as I could.

Including the Neighbors Kids

I was not only concerned about my own children being exposed but other children in the neighborhood. In addition to the things I did through our organization the Cooperettes, I personally did things on my own.

Wherever I was taking my own children someplace for some fun event, it seemed I always had a carload of neighbor children.

Once, when I found out that many children in the neighborhood had not been to the snow, I planned a trip to the mountains. I convinced Greyhound Bus to allow me to charter a bus for a neighborhood outing. I made a sign for the bus and called it a "Play date with DiJon," my youngest son. There were about forty neighborhood kids and a few other parents who went along. The kids had to have only $4.00 each, so that they could rent sleighs and toboggans. Some of the neighbor parents made food to take, and Duby made a big pot of chili beans for our winter picnic in the snow.

There were other activities that involved the teen's neighbor kids. There were always neighborhood kids at my house and activities in the backyard when we lived on Ninetieth Street in South Los Angeles. My daughter, Carol, would put on plays. I even helped Carol and her girlfriends organize a little social club so they could plan and pay for their own activities. I set up a bank account for them, and they raised money by having an admission price based on your waist size (one penny per inch).

I even had a community pride day. I got all of the kids in the neighborhood interested in keeping their property looking nice, so we had "Saturday Broom Sweeping Day" when all of the neighbor kids had to sweep the front of their houses. We did not wait on the Street Sweeper who did not always come to our street as often as they should have.

When a neighbor child got into trouble with the law. I would be the first there trying to help out, going to court to make sure that someone was there to support them. When my intervention did not prevent their incarceration, I kept in contact with them while they were incarcerated.

One example of this was a young neighbor kid, whose name I will withhold. He did not have the family support he needed and eventually found himself in trouble with the law. He was incarcerated for a long time. I obtained permission from the penal institution where he was incarcerated to allow me to mail with return paid postage library books to study for his high school diploma.

DiJon would check out library books, and we would send them to him to study. We did this back-and-forth until he graduated. We paid many a fine for late return books, but it was a pleasure because he finished high school and college in prison, and upon his release, he went on to become an accountant.

Gathering Other Children Along the Way

In addition to my own children, grand, and great-grandchildren, I have made other children my children by extension. Some are family friends, friends of my children, or others who have adopted me as their second mother, Godmother, or grandmother..

What I learned

I have learned that when you make children feel important, they respond in the most positive ways....

Do something for other kids who may not have the home environment that will provide them with the validation they need as growing and maturing children.

Provide noteworthy praise every opportunity you have.

As the saying goes "when a child lives with praise, they gain confidence." I have observed that children who are constantly criticized often seem to be unsure and hesitant.

It is important to know your children's friends and those with whom they associate. If you create an atmosphere where their friends feel comfortable in coming to your home you get to observe them firsthand without having to interrogate your kids about who they are hanging with. You may be surprised what you find out without prying when kids are freely interacting. Texting and being on social media and just hanging out may be what they like to do these days, but eating is still in style. Have them over to eat and hang at your place once in a while.

If you want your children to have nice friends and wholesome relationships, I learned that you have to involve yourself in their lives. I always had a house full of neighbor children visiting and to this very day many still tell me how much they appreciated me for that.

My Son and Daughter-in laws (Past or present)

I have always regarded and loved my daughters-in-law, Janice, Denice , and Ellen and my son-in-law Alvin as if they were my own children and have never sided with my own children against their spouses. I am a straight shooter, and if my children are in the wrong, and I find out, I have never hesitated in the least bit to let them know. I am fully aware that contemporary thinking is that parents should not become involved in their children affairs.

I agree wholeheartedly that you should not intermeddle. However, if you see a house on fire you don't just stand there if you have a watering hose. Your years of wisdom is the watering hose. Now, I agree that you must use the right approach. Firemen's don't just run in spraying water without first assessing the situation to determine how best to put out the fire without causing further damage or loss. If you are timid and don't know what to say or how to intervene, learn some conflict resolution skills. If you are young, take a conflict resolution class online. If you are old, listen to all of the great information given on the various self-help TV programs both religious and secular. I have learned and continue to learn so much about human behavior from just reading and watching various programs and most of all turning to the God within for guidance.

Denice	Janice	Alvin
(DiJon's wife)	*(Harold's former wife)*	*(Carol's former husband)*

What I learned

I have learned that your family can fall apart if you do nothing. I see parent's standing wringing their hands while their grown and married children's family falls apart when prayer, objective listening, and loving intervention would have helped to prevent that. You may not be helpful in all situations, because I have not been, but you never stop trying.

Not every burning house can be saved, but you still don't stop hosing it down.

Grandchildren

I have eight grandchildren. Ronnie's children: Windi, Shaka, Jana, and Mark. Carol's sons: C'Jay and stepson, Alvin Jr. (deceased). DiJon's children: Khari and Maleena. And grand-children-in-law: the spouse of Jana (Stanley) and the former spouse of Shaka (Shyrea).

I have an ongoing relationship with them all. Many of them confide in me about all kinds of personal issues because they still believe my advice is relevant (at least I hope that is why they confide in me). It's for sure I am going to share my wisdom in the matter whether they want it or not....

Harold's Children

| *Windi* | *Shaka* | *Jana* | *Mark* |

Carolyn' Children   *Di Jon's Children*

| *C'Jay* | *Alvin Jr.* (deceased) | *Maleena* | *Khari* |

Great-Grandchildren

I have nine great-grands: Shaka's children—Skye, Kinaya, Alim, and Klowie; and Jana's children—Stanley Jr., Giovanni, Jacob; and Mark's children—Diamond and Maurice.

Me with some of my Grand and Great-Grands December 2019

I have always tried to maintain a close relationship with each of them. I believe grandparents have a right to be involved in their grandchildren's lives, and I am adamant about exerting that right. When I feel the need to, I still get in my children's and grandchildren's faces, even at the ripe old age of ninety-plus, and I will even allow "the Josephine" to come out on them when I can no longer reason with them.

Sometimes you do wonder what impact you are having on your grandchildren, but when they seek you out to spend time with you, take walks with you; take you for doctor's appointment, make you a pancake breakfast, even willingly escort you to affairs, get the whole bunch together to celebrate your birthday or even get a note like the one below, it makes you feel that all of our cares and concerns are not in vain.

2-14-01

Dear Nana,

I hope you have a good Valentine's Day. I like the way you spend time with me and the way you cook too. I am glad you are around all the time, and thank you again for going on the field trip with me.

love
Khari

What I learned

Sure it takes a village to raise children, but before the village becomes involved, the family, including the extended family when at all possible, has to lay the foundation. I have been told on occasions by my children that "These are my children." But I am not the least bit bothered by this. I don't back off one bit because they are also my grandchildren, and grandparents do have rights. I have tried hard not to say or do anything contrary to what their parents are saying but try in my way to reinforce what is right. I have learned that if you do this in a loving way that your grandchildren will come to you.

I have also tried to find some nonintrusive way of always being involved in my grandchildren's lives for I can see that it pays high dividends. Just because you may not see the fruits of your involvement right away does not mean the seeds are not germinating. Some seeds lay dormant because it may be the winter of their lives. Don't give up; just pray for the springtime.

Dealing with Substance Abuse in the Family
Tough Love, Supportive love, but Always Love

Like many American parents and families, I was not spared from having to deal with a child addicted to substance. Although I did all that I thought I needed to do to prevent my children from falling prey to bad influence, My oldest son Harold (Ronnie)—during the sixties as he was trying to find his way—not only became actively involved with the activist movement in Los Angeles but along the way became chemically dependent, mainly on alcohol.

He has given me permission to share parts of his journey in hopes that it might help some family. He has also addressed some of this struggle in a recent book (Expression of Life) which he co-authored with The Creators Writer Group.

Ronnie was functionally dependent and maintained an appearance of sobriety by working and even attending short-term programs at local colleges and at times actively serving in the ministry. However, it was not long before the addiction eventually took its toll and cost him his marriage and family and the opportunity to utilize all of the wonderful potential he possessed as a bright, kind, and intellectual man.

After I got over my devastation and blaming myself like most parents do, especially on what was the underlying cause for the addiction, such as possibly how much he was affected by my divorce from his father whom he idolized. But then I would counter that notion with how I had given him every opportunity to do well that I could afford. Opportunities that many children wish they had and, how I and the rest of the family had given him lots of love, especially Mama and how we made sure that he did not lack for anything.

After this introspection activity was over, I got busy being very proactive seeking out all types of rehab facilities and treatment programs, which would work for a while, but soon Ronnie would relapse. I could see how hard he was trying to fight to stay sober by using all of the behavior modification approaches and techniques he had learned as well as leaning on his religious faith. It did hurt me to see him not be successful.

I am well aware that these approaches and techniques have worked for some people but not for most. Being the positive and motivational kind of person that I am, I never stopped preaching to him about "self-restraint and "where there is a will, there is a way. Even going so far as to use tough love by giving him many ultimatums about getting it together or else. The "or else" was far-reaching whatever I thought would make an impact.

Through it all I still had unconditional love, even though I was exasperated to say the least. Over a period of time of Ronnie's intermittent successes and failures, I began to immerse myself into whatever information I could find on the subject and have finally come to the realization that chemical dependency such as alcoholism and other drug related dependency are a disease like other chronic disease such as diabetes.

You would never tell a person diagnosed with diabetes or some other chronic disease not to seek a physical or medical cure or say to them to just use will power or try a series of behavior modification techniques or just simply attend meetings. Not that any of these things are not good however these things alone will not treat a physical dependency. Obviously, the goal for curing chemical dependency is abstinence, but you have to first get to abstinence. There are many excellent treatments programs, one's own faith, and other self-help groups that can assist and are available and should be sought out early on in the disease process.

Like myself, Ronnie's friends never deserted him, his pastor and friend was always there for the both of us. This spoke volumes to me about the real and good person Ronnie is.

Victory at Last

I never gave up on my son, and now I have lived to see him achieve sobriety.

Ronnie is faithful in attending his support sessions daily sometimes morning and night. He is committed in maintaining his sobriety. I am so grateful to God and so proud of his courage as I watch him try so hard to make amends to his children and grandchildren and being involved in their lives to the degree they will allow him. He is very involved in his church and especially in the youth activities of the church.

Like me he never misses the opportunity to show some "Act of kindness" to people with whom he comes in contact.

What I learned

We should treat people with chemical dependency with the same sense of urgency and concern that we treat people with diabetes, heart failure, or obesity or any other chronic disease. We get them treatment.

Help them find a professional support system if you cannot be one or because you have become exasperated with their behavior.

I learn that we do not need to be ashamed or talk in quiet whispers about a member of our family suffering from substance abuse, just like we are not shamed when someone in our family is suffering from diabetes or another chronic disease.

While you help them seek treatment whether you decide that you must use "tough love or gentle love, use love. As the scripture says "Love covers a multitude of sins."

So never give up believing that with help, especially, I found with the help of God, sobriety is possible.

Family Reunion

The older I became the more significant I came to understand the importance of family reunions and have regretted not having been involved in my own family reunions until later in life.

I believe that family reunions are important no matter the race or culture, but as a woman of color, I have come to a greater understanding of family reunions among African Americans.

The importance of the family reunion among African Americans can best be summarized as written by Renee McCoy in her article published in the American Journal on Aging. Her article titled "Elders, Cultural Traditions and the Family Reunion" provides the following overview:

> Family reunions are important rituals that have long contributed to the survival, health, and endurance of African American families, helping to maintain cultural heritage even in uncertain and turbulent times. Although there is variation in how African Americans hold family reunions these days, some key elements remain constant. One constant is that these events generate such power, in large part, from the participation of the elders—the keepers of the African American legacy. ww.asaging.org/blog/African-American-elders-cultural – by Renee McCoy. Retrieved Oct. 2015

Being an only child and not having siblings you also don't have nieces and nephews. My stepsister Beatrice had no children and my stepbrother I only saw once. I only had aunts, uncles, and cousins. Most relatives I knew were from my mother's family. Mama was from a big family of thirteen.

Although as a child I visited with my family who were most in my birth state Louisiana however after relocating to California in my early teens, I only saw a cousin or relative if they came to California so many of my younger relatives not of my generation I have come to know in the last thirty years.

So I had to make every effort to reintegrate myself in the family and now have come to be one of the oldest family matriarchs.

The family's branches are primarily Coleman and Walker. I am from the Coleman branch. There is also branch overlapping as some Coleman sisters married Walker brothers. I have embraced every family member I have met whether Walker or Coleman, and I am loving it.

I have attended by now at least eight family reunions and actually helped to host the 2000 year Turn of the Century one held in Los Angeles. I am always amazed to see how much the younger generation are intrigued with finding out about their roots and who they are kin to. It is often difficult to get teenagers or young adults in much, but if you tell them it's a family reunion, they are all for it. It is that natural curiosity in knowing yourself and who you are kin to.

It has become very important to me to have my family know their extended family. Better late than never. Wanting to know your ancestry is a natural phenomenon. There are industries making millions on providing people with their genealogy. It is such a good feeling when someone walks up and says I am your cousin or we are kin.

There are family members who have provided the family with some genealogy, which has been helpful but more is needed. Perhaps some reading this book will take up the mantle.

Coleman Walker Family Elders

Orlean (Coleman)   *Jeff Walker*   *Leatha (Coleman) Walker*

What I learned

What I have learned is that we were placed in families for a reason. We didn't get to choose. Perhaps you are placed there to provide guidance, inspiration, wisdom, or even family history. Family reunions should be a time of finding out how you can shine your light. The Holy Scripture said that if you have a light you don't put it under a bush but a high place where others can see your good.... Perhaps we are put there to be a light.

Often, I hear that our people have low "self-esteem" and it makes me angry. Self-esteem is tied into feeling good about yourself, knowing who you are, where you came from, and who you are connected or related to. Some young people are looking outside their families because they do not know that right in their own family there are many who have accomplished much. We fail when we do not make an effort to help them find out.

I have learned that it is our responsibility as elders to ensure that our young hear not only about the struggle but about the overcomers. They need to know about the inventers and discoverers, astronauts, educators, artists, along with entertainers, and sport figures.

Let them know that there are and the many patents for inventions that we were given credit for as a people and many others we were not.For all families Black, white, Asian, Hispanic—we owe it to posterity to find out if we don't know and "pass it on." Some die with the history still in them without ever passing it on not even in anecdotal form.

Chapter 18

Enjoying
Growing Older

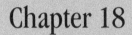

I am grateful to live a long time, but I refuse to be "old." Now the study of gerontology includes ways to stay healthy and keep the body young and active. At ninety-six, I am in overall good physical and mental health. I have not had any serious or long-term illnesses in my life. I have been blessed without having any serious illnesses. Almost fifty years ago, I had a bout with Meniere's disease (an inner ear disorder) and in 2014 a bout with sciatica. Other than that, I have had almost perfect health. God's Favor and to "God be the Glory"

I still try to stay fit. Before I get out of the bed each morning, I start my exercise program. I do bicycle exercises with my legs while I am still in bed as a warmup and until the age of ninety-five, I walked at least one mile every day. I still walk almost every day, but I have cut down somewhat at my children's insistence.

When I was eighty-seven on one occasion, I was walking up a steep hill and several young men in their thirties or forties were walking a distance behind me and could not see my face. I was dressed in a sweat suit that showed off my still shapely body. Thinking I was a younger woman they shouted, "Mama, You are looking good." I turned around and said, "I guess so for an eighty-seven-year-old." They were shocked and quickly start apologizing. "We are so sorry, ma'am. We did not mean any disrespect." I thought to myself and no disrespect taken. The truth is, it was a compliment.

At ninety-five I was still driving often. I got my driver's license renewed in 2016 at the age of ninety-four. I still do my own marketing, and until age ninety-five drove neighbors when needed to appointments and to church. I still attend many social events now mainly at my daughter's insistence.

Orlean and Dr. Burnett (2012)

I was seeing a dear friend, Dr. Cleophus Barnett socially until his death in 2014. I enjoyed having a social companion to take me dancing and to other family and social events. I think that until you are dead you should enjoy living.

I stay as current as I possibly can in both my dress and activities. (I still love beautiful clothes.) I still love dancing. I don't text, but as I mentioned earlier, I did take a computer class in my eighties. You can't do anything about aging, but you can do something about being old.

Despite what some of my grandchildren may think, I am not rich. I do live comfortably but that is because of my hard work and trying to manage whatever resources I have. But most of all because I am blessed of God and have favor and belief with all my heart "where there is a will there is a way."

Travel

In my early life, I did not get to do international traveling, so in my late seventies, I decided it was time to change this. I know that travel broadens your perception about the world and the world's people. So far I have visited Israel, Greece, Italy, and others. I understand that for some people it is not important, however I hope that my grandchildren and great grandchildren and those young people in my life will value its importance.

Everyone should want to see at least some of this magnificent earth before leaving it. You don't need to be rich to travel. If you really want to travel, don't say I don't have anyone to go with me. There are all kinds of groups you can travel with. I went with my church group. Many people spend the amount of money it takes to travel on various types of entertainment and as we say in Los Angeles, "they spend that much money on a trip to Vegas." Some will say that they are too old. I recently read how people are paying younger travel companions to go with them. Remember "where there is a will there is a way."

Stella Oceanis : Sun Line Cruises

Bon Voyage Orlean

Meeting the President

I have lived through the terms of sixteen Presidents of the United States. Namely, Calvin Coolidge, Herbert Hoover, Franklin D. Roosevelt, Harry Truman, Dwight D. Eisenhower, John F. Kennedy, Lyndon B. Johnson, Richard Nixon, Gerald Ford, Jimmy Carter, Ronald Regan, George Herbert Bush, William J. Clinton, George W. Bush, Barack Obama, and now Donald Trump. Eight Democrats and eight Republicans.

I pray my children and especially grandchildren never forget to realize the power of the vote for which many gave up their lives and liberty. Nor the power of peaceful protest for I have witnessed that both can bring needed change.

Although I never met Martin Luther King, I have lived to see the result of his legacy. I have witnessed the country be to the right, left, and center and through it all, it was necessary to stay focused on what you can do to make your life and community better for yourself and others.

I am grateful that I lived to see the country elect a Black President. It was almost impossible to believe. Perhaps we will elect a woman as president in my lifetime.

Meeting President Obama

Orlean and President Obama (California)

The only president that I had met before meeting President Obama was President Clinton and Presidential Candidate Robert Kennedy. My daughter carol received an invitation for President Obama's Inaugural Ball and took me as one of her guest

I was so appreciative to be in the same room with the president and to take pictures with the First Lady. I also accompanied my daughter back to a White House Dinner with the President and First Lady, which was a more intimate setting. More recently I finally got that picture with President Obama when I attended a fundraising with my daughter Carol here in California. This was one of the highlights of my life.

My first thought was what if Mama could have lived to see a Black (bi-racial) president and to meet President Obama. I believe that history will treat what he was able to accomplish favorably. Having lived through sixteen presidents and staying politically aware, I do know something about presidents and politics.

My Daughter Carol, President Obama and Me

What I learned

First I learned that it's not all about genes. If you want to keep living, you have to keep moving. Some form of physical exercise is a must.

Second, I learned that staying relevant means having a purpose. Perhaps it means lending your expertise to a up-and-comer in a position, craft, trade or profession you left, or volunteering either in person or virtual. I manage to do this over the phone or impromptu on my morning walk.

I learned that there is richness in investing in the young. Your grandchildren or maybe someone else's grandchildren. Not all of your talks and pearls of wisdom will fall on deaf ears.. Something you said or shared might just stick and make a difference. In addition, try something new like travel if you have not and met new people. It will enrich your life. It has mine.

During my life I have lived through the term of sixteen presidents.

What I have learned is that no matter who is president, God is still on the throne. From what I know scripturally, God does not care one bit about our political persuasion or our petty partisan politics. What he does care about is the current state of Man's inhumanity to Man. How we treat each other.

Chapter 19

My Faith

*B*ecause of Mama's teaching, I always felt that God was with me no matter what and, as Mama so aptly put it "God will never leave you alone." I put my faith in that, and it has carried me through it all. I did not really understand the role of the Holy Spirit in my life, even though I could feel His presence. Although I had attended church all of my life, I never really understood all of the Biblical principles available to me as a child of God.

However, this was about to change. In the '70s, there was a new kid on the block. A new spiritual teacher taking LA by storm. His name—Fredrick K. C. Price. People from all over and from many different denominations stood in line every Sunday just to get inside to hear him. Eventually he was on television and appealing to a broader and larger audience.

I had never been to a church where I had to take my Bible. But there I was with more enthusiasm about really learning the Bible than I had ever had before. Now I came to know from Pastor Price as he referred to himself (Not Reverend) more about this presence that had guided me all my life as the Holy Spirit and that I could have a personal relationship with Him. His teachings helped me to confirmed how my Faith in God and his Son Jesus had allowed me to always speak and believe that I could have what I said. It also helped me to understand the favor of God, which I always seemed to have.

You could tell who was listening to his messages because they had no problem with saying probably for the first time in their life "Praise the Lord" it was now in vogue. You could not even call people on the telephone any more without hearing "Praise the Lord" in their message. Everybody attending his church seemed to be repeating and sharing Pastor Price's message from the Sunday before.

Even at our clothing shop as women were getting all dolled up for a special occasion, there was a sharing of the message they had heard with the intermittent "Praise the Lord" without hesitation or embarrassment, which was unheard of before now. What an impact Pastor Price made on the spiritual growth of the community and especially in my life.

The other unforgettable influence in my spiritual growth on a more personal level came from a young Minister Beverly Crawford, (Bam) who eventually became like one of my children.

What I learned

I learned that we were not left on this earth alone. Upon leaving Jesus said to his disciples "I will ask the Father, and he will give you another advocate to help you forever, the Spirit of Truth". John 14:15-17

I learned that we must use this ready Helper. Guide and Advocate when making decisions, feeling helpless and needing comfort

Second, I learned that "Faith without works is dead."

LEAP AND THE NET WILL APPEAR

Chapter 20

My Life's Purpose

When you are young you wonder about your purpose for living. However, when you get older the purpose becomes very clear at least for me it has. I truly believe that we are our brother's keeper. When Jesus was asked what was the greatest commandment, he said was: Thou shall love the Lord thy God with all thy heart, and with all thy soul, and with thy entire mind. This is the first and great commandment. And the second is like unto it, Thou shalt love thy neighbor as thyself. (Matthew 22:37-38) KJV

My purpose is to help people where I can to live a better life and to reach their goals. I am always trying to encourage people through sharing my life's experience or through something good or motivational that I might have heard or read about. I do this in my daily life either in person on the phone, on my morning walk, at the market, or any place I come into contact with people especially the young.

I have not only just given advice; I have also tried to help with whatever resources I have based on the belief that "I am my brother's keeper."

Earlier in life as I spoke of in a previous chapter, I founded a charitable organization (The Cooperettes) to help those in need, and I have worked hard to make a difference in the community.

My greatest emphasis when sharing with the young is that they must get a good education. I have come to see that life is not too kind for most of those who do not receive formal schooling; obviously there are a few exceptions but not many.

I am always espousing my concern for an education in words and deeds. Whenever I have the opportunity, especially with young people, even if it is the kid packing my grocery bag. I am always inquiring about what they are doing with their life and offer advice even when they may not see that they need it.

Being your brother's keeper does not just mean providing tangible goods; it means also "providing a soft place for people to land." Hundreds of people over my lifetime have honored me with their confidence about issues and problems concerning their personal struggles, challenges, hopes, and dreams and have never had to worry about if I would keep their confidence.

I like how Sandol Stoddard stated it in the *Children's Bible* she authored. She said that Jesus in his teaching the Beatitudes said that "God's children are the Salt of the earth, with you he can preserve his treasures, without you how can he season anything."

Understanding "The Will"

I strongly believed in the saying that "where there is a will there is a way." Sometimes this strong belief has driven me to do almost the impossible. This belief has also caused me to become impatient with people who can't seem to embrace the concept.

My impatience has to do with knowing that it works. I have seen how this worked in Mama's life and in my own life. So during my difficulties, restriction, barriers, hard times, discrimination, abandonment, rejection, heartbreak, divorce, and marriage I was able to overcome believing "where there is a will to overcome, there is a way."

There is no promise that you will not have trials and tribulations. Jesus speaks saying "These things I have spoken to you, that in me you might have peace. In the world you shall have tribulation: but be of good cheer; I have overcome the world." John 16:33 MEV (Modern English Version).

My will versus God's will

I never have wanted my will to be different from God's will for my life, however, I am sure there were times that I thought that I did, and it was during these times I ran into road blocks. I soon realized that God's will is a perfect will, so it is better to fall in line with his will rather than my oftentimes imperfect will.

What I learned

I learn that you must find purpose in life, and once you have identified that purpose you must pursue it with zeal. You can achieve that purpose for where there is a will there is a way.

I believe your epitaph should be that you did something no matter how small to make a positive difference in the life of others. That you did not just come onto this earth to take up space.

I also learned to ask for God's will and not my own for His will is perfect.

I also learned in these ninety-six years that it's all about faith in the Creator and next in yourself. I always had lots of self-confidence, and I now understand the saying that "If a child lives with praise, he/she will grow into a confident person." I relished in praise, and it made me confident. Make sure to give noteworthy praise to your children and other young people around you, and it will boost their confidence and perhaps they can embody my tenet "where there is a will, there is a way."

Being Recognized by the Community

Over the years various groups and organizations have recognized me for what they see as noteworthy. It is both wonderful and humbling to be recognized.

Among the many awards and recognitions are: Outstanding Business Women of the Year from Iota Phi Lambda Sorority, Inc., One of the Ten Outstand Women of The Year by the LA Sentinel Newspaper, Black Business and Professional Women of LA County and recognition by the YWCA, The Negro College Fund, Wives of Bench and Bar, Black Women Network and Rejected Stone Christian Fellowship.

Some of Orleans's many awards and Recognition

I am also blessed with wonderful neighbors I love and who love me. They often leave me little notes of appreciation and sometimes just simple greetings attached to a bag or basket of "goodies" on my front porch.

What I learned

In these ninety-six years, I have learned that whether you wish to or not that when you leave this earth, you will leave a legacy. What will it be? A legacy can be good or bad and you are orchestrating it each day you live. It is amazing to me that your past, no matter how glorious or not, is not as important as your present or your future.

I learn not to waste time harping on what I did in the past. Although I had to reflect for the purpose of this book, I do not ordinarily spend time in the past. As long as you are alive you are working on that legacy.

What it will be is up to us. I have learned that every day I start on a new slate and that God is faithful and will never leave or forsake me and where there is a will to write something good on this clean slate there is a way. I know that I did not come to this earth to just take up space but to accomplish something in life.

Chapter 21

About the Author

Eunice Giles Morgan Walker, RN, MSN, JD

About the Author:

Eunice Giles Morgan Walker, RN, MSN, JD

Eunice is a Lawyer, Registered Nurse, and Certified Mediator who works as a Legal Healthcare Management Consultant, Leadership and Management Coach, Mediator, Strategic Planner and Post-Graduate Educator. She is also an avid Grant Writer and a longtime friend and relative of Orlean Dubuclet.

Orlean, age 96 with the Book's Author